MARTIN BOOTH

111 PLACES IN BATH THAT YOU SHOULDN'T MISS

Photographs by Barbara Evripidou

emons:

For Joanna

Martin Booth

For Ainley and Diana Wade

Barbara Evripidou

Cäcilienstraße 48, 50667 Köln
info@emons-verlag.de

Layout: Conny Laue, based on a design by Lübbeke | Naumann | Thoben
Maps: altancicek.design, www.altancicek.de
Basic cartographical information from Openstreetmap,
© OpenStreetMap-Mitwirkende, OdbL
QR code notice: External content is provided via Google Maps.
Google's privacy policy applies.
Edited by Ros Horton
Printing and binding: sourc-e GmbH
Printed in Europe 2026
ISBN 978-3-7408-2871-4

Guidebooks for Locals & Experienced Travellers
Join us in uncovering new places around the world at
www.111places.com

FOREWORD

When SouthGate shopping centre was being built, detractors called it a Georgian theme park. This is a criticism that could be levelled at much of Bath. There is no finer example anywhere in the world of Georgian town planning, using the undulating landscape to spectacular effect. What had been a small medieval walled town became a resort devoted to leisure with buildings among England's most fashionable. Has this distinct style been faithfully preserved or has it been pickled? That will be up to you to decide as you navigate Bath's steep contours, dodging Jane Austen re-enactors as you proceed.

But focusing too much on these gorgeous Georgians – however much their influence still pervades – does Bath a disservice. Of course, this is a Roman city as well. The reminders of Aquae Sulis are everywhere and it is one of the reasons why UNESCO has designated the entirety of Bath as a World Heritage Site. Venice is the only other European city to hold that honour.

Remove the Georgians and the Romans and you still have a city that may have been small but which more than 1,000 years ago was important enough to see the first king of all England crowned in its abbey. Leap forward into living memory and Bath's flourishing industry saw everything from huge cranes to millions of books manufactured and printed here before being sent around the world.

While writing this book, I have walked and cycled around the city; and around and around Old Down Cycle Track. I have spoken to proud residents, hard-working business owners and award-winning baristas; all ensuring that today's Bath is as unique and special as it has been for a millennium and more. To distil a city as multi-faceted as this into 111 chapters is an a near-impossible task but I hope you will use this book to – in true Emons fashion – go off the beaten track and discover Bath for the first time, or rediscover a familiar place afresh.

FAVOURITE TOURS

Bath is an eminently walkable city with many attractions packed into what was once a small walled settlement. Much of the city centre has been pedestrianised and more areas of the wider city are also seeing traffic-calming measures introduced. Be sure to explore further afield on a bicycle – but be prepared for more than a few hills.

A WALK AROUND THE WALLS

This walk follows the surviving route of Bath's former Roman wall, which has mostly disappeared but whose ancient route is still followed by a few of today's roads. The name Upper Borough Walls is a clue that this was once the northernmost stretch of the wall. Start at its junction with Trim Bridge to find a few parish boundary markers (ch. 63) which still share the wall's delineation. Close by is a well-preserved fragment of the wall (ch. 53). Stay on Upper Borough Walls and walk by what in 1742 opened as Bath General Hospital (ch. 54) and later became the Mineral Water Hospital. Look for more parish boundary markers on the walls beyond Magalleria (ch. 51). Cross Northgate Street (another clue!) and onto Bridge Street with Mallory now occupying the site of the former St Mary by the North Gate Church. The route of the wall passes through Guildhall Market next to which is the surviving Eastgate (ch. 28). Orange Grove and the Prince of Orange obelisk (ch. 69) would have been just within the wall that now follows Terrace Walk and Old Orchard Street on which is the former Theatre Royal (ch. 60). The long-gone South Gate was located close to where Southgate Street joins Stall Street. Walk along Lower Borough Walls, near to that are the Road Peace Memorial (ch. 75) and Chapel Arts Centre (ch. 18). The Chapel of St Michael Within, part of St John's Foundation (ch. 78), is so-called because it was within the walls that now follow Westgate Buildings (yes, another clue) and Saw Close until joining Upper Borough Walls.

GEORGIAN GRANDEUR

Bath was almost completely transformed from the 1720s and this walk will explore the Georgian grandeur for which the city is still famous. Start at Pulteney Radial Gate (ch. 70) for a splendid view of Pulteney Bridge, one of only four bridges in the world to have shops across its full span on both sides (ch. 9). Turn left along Grand Parade to Parade Gardens, laid out in 1709. On nearby Orange Grove is an obelisk (ch. 69) commemorating the cure in Bath in 1734 of the Prince of Orange. Walk up High Street and Northgate Street, veering left at Broad Street to see a plaque to Dr Oliver (ch. 27), who invented his eponymous biscuit in around 1750. Turn left along Green Street, Quiet Street and Wood Street to Queen Square, with Queen's Parade Place to its north featuring two sedan chair houses (ch. 79). Unfortunately there are no sedans operating today so continue on foot along Gravel Walk (ch. 34) mentioned in Jane Austen's *Persuasion*, passing the Georgian Garden (ch. 33) before reaching the architectural showpiece of Royal Crescent.

ON TWO WHEELS

It was once where steam trains travelled from Bath towards Bournemouth and now Combe Down Tunnel is one of the longest cycling and walking tunnels in the UK. Find it on the Two Tunnels Greenway (ch. 100), which is best traversed by bicycle. Head by Brickfields Park (ch. 16) before first entering Devonshire Tunnel and then Combe Down Tunnel, close to whose southern portal is Tucking Mill Viaduct (ch. 98). Leave the Two Tunnels Greenway here and head east along Tucking Mill Lane towards Monkton Combe, stopping to see its lock-up (ch. 55). Continue along Church Lane, cross Brassknocker Hill and you will reach Dundas Aqueduct. Now head north along the Kennett & Avon Canal towpath back to the city centre, but not before first finding Claverton Pumping Station (ch. 21), Warleigh Weir (ch. 105), Cafe on the Barge (ch. 17) and Widcombe Lock Flight (ch. 107).

111 PLACES

Scan here for
the digital map

1 A. H. Hale

A 200-year-old former apothecary with heraldic heritage

A. H. Hale – or Hale's to most Bathonians – has traded in this same spot near Pulteney Bridge since 1826 within one of the city's earliest specially built retail premises. One of the UK's oldest dispensing chemists was originally an apothecary's shop and those days come vividly to life with a selection of potions (sorry: medicines) displayed in glass jars both in the shop window and on the shelves inside.

Run by the Doshi family and once also an opticians, the business is officially called The Bathwick Pharmacy and although it might appear old fashioned, it is a fully functioning pharmaceutical emporium; just one where you can also buy your grandma's favourite perfume while picking up your prescription. Jane Austen's mother, Cassandra, was treated here when she was gravely ill, and the pharmacy has a copy of the poem she wrote to thank the then-owners for the medicine that helped in her recovery.

Looking down on passers-by from above the Ionic columns is a colourful coat of arms featuring real gold leaf. If the insignia doesn't look familiar, that's because this is the royal warrant of Charlotte Sophia, the wife of King George III. The coat of arms is thought to have been commissioned in 1817 when Queen Charlotte was in Bath, coincidentally when she heard the tragic news of the death of her beloved daughter Princess Charlotte in childbirth. Made out of Coade stone, it was first put on display at a business now unknown that wanted to display its royal seal of approval. The lion, unicorn and crest were not originally here, however, having been found in the basement of a shop on Milsom Street in the 1950s. Given to the city council, it was then thought to have been decorated by pupils at Kingswood School and was stored in the Guildhall until a previous owner of A. H. Hale offered to restore and reposition it in its current location in 1982.

ADDRESS 8 Argyle Street, BA2 4BQ, +44 (0)1225 464429 TIP If coats of arms are your jam, then the City of Bath Heraldic Society (www.bath-heraldry.org.uk) is for you. The group meets regularly at Manvers Street Baptist Church Hall to talk all things ensign, escutcheon and insignia.

2 American Museum & Gardens

A slice of the States

The only one of its kind outside the USA, the American Museum contains decorative arts from the United States and the wider North American continent. 'By showcasing different perspectives and how cultures influence one another, we aim to entertain, inform and inspire,' says the museum's website. There are more than 12,000 objects in the museum's permanent collection from a 'patchwork paradise' of American quilts to furniture and maps. Previous exhibitions have included such varied themes of space exploration, dinosaurs and Lego. And then there are the surrounding gardens that feature two and a half acres of formal garden. Keep a lookout too for the Children's Garden, arboretum, parkland and woodland walk.

In recent years, the museum's trustees have questioned their collections, in particular the items made by Indigenous North Americans that mostly consist of objects specifically created to sell to tourists. These followed techniques and used the same materials as earlier pieces 'but they are not imbued with the same spiritual or religious importance and were intended to leave the communities where they were made'. Alongside centuries-old basketwork, pottery and beadwork are now newer pieces by contemporary Indigenous artists.

The story of the American Museum itself started through a transatlantic alliance between American psychiatrist Dr Dallas Pratt and British-born John Judkyn, an antiques dealer who became a US citizen. After searching the UK for suitable premises, the pair purchased Claverton Manor and first opened their museum to the public in 1961 with the ambition to showcase American decorative arts 'and dispel stereotypes of American culture'. Panelling and floors were shipped over to Britain from the States, with reconstructions of demolished buildings created within the house that dates back to 1820.

ADDRESS Claverton Manor, BA2 7BD, +44 (0)1225 460503, www.americanmuseum.org TIP Hollywood is a regular visitor to Bath. Look out for familiar sites in films including *Les Misérables*, *The Duchess* and *Vanity Fair*.

3 Bath Boating Station

Messing about on the river

'Believe me, my young friend, there is nothing – absolutely nothing – half so much worth doing as simply messing about in boats.' So said the Water Rat to the Mole in *The Wind in the Willows* by Kenneth Grahame, and he was absolutely right. If he visited Bath, the place he would go for whimsical watery pleasure would be Bath Boating Station, a charming Victorian boating station on the picturesque banks of the River Avon. You don't need any experience to hire a vessel here. Olympic rowers are just as welcome as complete novices as you book a boat for one or two hours to explore the river. Choose either a rowing boat, canoe or punt and after your strenuous efforts, reward yourself with a picnic in the grounds if you haven't already tucked into your sandwiches on the river.

If you want to make your visit to Bath Boating Station last more than the maximum two hours, there are four properties on site to rent, each of which sleeps two adults. Quote Kenneth Grahame to your heart's content at Toad Hall, the smallest of the four but which still has a riverside balcony. There is also the Garden Room, the Apartment and – the best of the lot – Swan House, which even has its own sitting room and conservatory as well as a balcony overlooking the river and the gardens. During the boating season, guests are often allowed to enjoy a free afternoon's boating.

Just downstream from Bath Boating Station is Cleveland Pools, the UK's oldest public outdoor swimming pool. Built in 1815 but closed in 1984, it had a remarkable resurrection following decades of effort from a passionate group of volunteers and campaigners. The much-loved Georgian lido on the banks of the River Avon reopened in September 2023 to much fanfare but closed just four months later after flooding caused substantial damage to the 'flood-proof' plant room, and in 2026 it sadly remains closed behind a locked gate.

ADDRESS Bath Boating Station, Forrester Road, BA2 6QE, www.bathboating.co.uk
TIP Above the boating station within the former rowing clubhouse is The Bathwick Boatman restaurant (www.bathwickboatman.com) run by husband and wife team Ben and Rosy Hall.

4 Bath City Farm

Pigs in the city

The land that Bath City Farm is on was mentioned in the Domesday Book and it is likely that there has been farming on this site for thousands of years. So the team at the working farm are continuing a long legacy. They celebrated their 30th anniversary as a charitable organisation in 2025, with their mission today to be 'a welcoming urban farm using our unique setting and targeted projects to educate, improve wellbeing and transform lives. Our vision is to create a healthy community rooted in nature, food, farming and each other'.

The farm (previously a dairy farm where you could bring your own jug to buy milk) covers 37 acres on a hill with wonderful views across the city. As well as being a working farm, it contains woodland and nature trails, a children's adventure play area made from wood and tyres, a café for breakfasts and lunches, an amphitheatre, ponds and community garden plots. On the hillside are several natural springs and each field has its own traditional name such as Lower Lamb Sleight – 19th-century monikers once lost due to a lack of use but now reinstated. Look out for a crater caused by a bomb that fell on the land during the Bath Blitz.

Entrance is free but donations are exceedingly welcome, with money going towards the farm's charitable side, including the work their team do with people living with mental health concerns, additional learning needs and other complex needs. You can also buy some feed for £1 a bag in order to feed the farm's herd of hungry pygmy goats, or the chickens and ducks if you prefer feathered rather than furry friends. Look out too for pigs, cows, rare breeds of sheep and Shetland pony duo Dougie and Dougal, whose favourite thing to do is chasing the sheep. Don't become too attached to many of these animals, however, as some are bred for meat with farm-reared pork and lamb products for sale in the café.

ADDRESS Bath City Farm, Kelston View, Whiteway, BA2 1NW, +44 (0)1225 481269, www.bathcityfarm.org.uk TIP If you love alpacas, book a visit to Bell Farm (www.bellfarmalpacas.co.uk) for a walking experience, an Alpaca Meet & Greet or a picnic with the South American camelids.

5 The Bath Press

Once Bath's biggest employer

Look on your bookshelves at home and you could well have a tome that was printed at the Bath Press. Or you might know how to write in shorthand, which also has an intriguing link with this corner of the city. *Diana: Her True Story* by Andrew Morton was printed here in 1992 and one year later, Margaret Thatcher's *The Downing Street Years* rolled off the presses on the Lower Bristol Road. What was once Bath's biggest employer first opened here in 1889 and the five-acre site was only vacated in 2007.

While the book you're reading was being printed in 2026 (in Germany rather than Bath), the site was in the process of being turned into hundreds of new homes and offices. All that remains of what used to be a sprawling set of industrial buildings is the 1920s façade and a chimney, not listed but now a 'non-designated heritage asset' following previous plans that would have demolished it.

The Bath Press was the name of the company when this site was closed, but when it opened, it was the Pitman Press printing works that had been founded by Isaac Pitman (1813–1897) of eponymous shorthand fame. And a bonus fun fact: the inventor of the world's most widely used system of shorthand was also vice president of the Vegetarian Society. Born in Trowbridge in Wiltshire, he trained as a teacher and invented his system of shorthand – originally known as stenographic sound-hand – in 1837. He moved to Bath soon after the invention that would make him famous and opened his first Phonetic Institute, the fifth iteration of which was on the site of his printing works. Pitman only originally began printing in order to make his educational publications as widely available as possible. He was also a keen advocate for spelling reform, wanting to adopt a phonetic system to simplify English orthography. This proved less successful than his shorthand but he was still knighted by Queen Victoria in 1894.

ADDRESS The Bath Press, Lower Bristol Road, BA2 3EJ TIP To mark Sir Isaac Pitman's legacy, the University of Bath has a dedicated collection of materials relating to shorthand, writing systems, phonetics and the language of communication (www.bath.ac.uk/corporate-information/pitman-collection).

6 Bath River Line

Following the River Avon through the heart of Bath

New York's High Line, a public park constructed on a former elevated freight line in Manhattan, has been an inspiration across the world. Bath's new 'line' is an ambitious scheme in the planning for several years. Its first phase of construction from Windsor Bridge to Green Park started in 2025 and includes new seating, improved access to the river path and 'pollinator-friendly planting'. Bath River Line project aims to create a 10 kilometre (6 mile) 'linear park' (not to be confused with Bath's existing Linear Park) following the River Avon through the heart of the city. It's not 10 kilometres in total, but rather a collection of spots along the water that will eventually stretch from Batheaston to Newbridge. Funding for phase one comes from the West of England Mayoral Combined Authority and the UK Social Prosperity Fund.

Look out for phase one works in Green Park; in the north west and south east corners of Norfolk Crescent green space; on the riverside path to the south of Bath Artists' Studios; at the junction of the steps from Norfolk Buildings Road; to the south of Norfolk Buildings; and to the north and south of Midland Bridge.

At the beginning of building, Bath & North East Somerset's cabinet member for climate and sustainable travel, Sarah Warren, said that Bath River Line 'will help to expand the active travel network in Bath by creating a level, accessible route for everyone to use while the new seating spaces and planting will help to improve biodiversity and climate change resilience and provide social spaces that can be enjoyed by residents and visitors'.

Quoted in the project's community consultation, one local resident summed up the mood of many users of the sometimes very narrow path next to the river: 'When I'm a cyclist I'm annoyed by pedestrians and when I'm a pedestrian I'm annoyed by cyclists'. Their views on the improvements are unknown.

ADDRESS Bath River Line will eventually stretch from Batheaston to Newbridge, www.bathnes.gov.uk/bath-river-line TIP Dozens of artists are based at Bath Artists' Studios (www.bathartistsstudios.org) on Comfortable Place, which also offers numerous weekly classes in a variety of disciplines.

7 Bath Royal Literary & Scientific Institution

Inspiring minds for 200 years

The Bath Royal Literary & Scientific Institution is just that: an institution. Founded in 1824, it is 'a place where science, literature and the arts come together to fire up imaginations and showcase amazing collections of treasures from around the world'. For one weekend during their bicentenary year in 2024, the BRLSI spilled outdoors onto Queen Square for a free festival, but usually their events take place inside and online.

During Black History Month in 2025, National Trust curator Dr Tim Moore explored the vibrant histories of people of colour in Georgian-era Bath; and social activist Roger Griffith took attendees on a journey to Bath's neighbouring city to see how the 1963 Bristol Bus Boycott changed the face of Britain. Other recent talks have explored subjects including Jane Austen, people trafficking, queer Georgians, the war in Ukraine and the RNLI (which was also founded in 1824). Among the permanent displays is the first extra-terrestrial object collected and described on Earth: a piece of a four-billion-year-old meteorite that landed in Siberia in 1779.

From its earliest days, the BRLSI has hosted lectures and exhibitions of its collections of archaeology, ethnology, zoology, mineralogy, botany and palaeontology. Its original building on Terrace Walk was demolished as part of a road development scheme in 1932 and soon after moving to Queen Square, all of their collections had to go into storage as the Admiralty requisitioned their new headquarters. In 1992, the grand old institution was relaunched as a charity following a campaign against plans to disperse its collections, and since then 'has continued to celebrate the past, present and future of Bath and the world', as a mural in Parade Gardens close to its first home explains.

ADDRESS Bath Royal Literary & Scientific Institution, 16 Queen Square, BA1 2HN, +44 (0)1225 312084, www.brlsi.org TIP Next to Queen Square on Queen's Parade is the Bath & County Club (www.bathandcountyclub.com), a historic private members' club whose headquarters are usually covered in foliage.

8 Bath Spa Railway Station

Covering your tracks

Bath was more than 150 years from being granted World Heritage status when plans were first drawn up for a railway between Bristol and London. If this was modern-day Bath, however, there might well have been consternation from UNESCO towards the Great Western Railway's chief engineer, Isambard Kingdom Brunel, who did nothing to ensure his new station would blend in. Unlike the termini at Temple Meads and Paddington, many of Brunel's other stations were smaller in scale and ambition, and given the nickname 'Brunel's barns'. But Bath Spa is by no means modest. Nor is it complementary in style, unlike the 'Georgian theme park' of SouthGate shopping centre opposite the station that almost caused Bath to be stripped of its World Heritage status. It also has noticeably more space between its tracks than many other stations due to Brunel originally adopting the wider broad gauge before moving to standard gauge in 1892, with a glazed roof once spanning the platforms.

In Sydney Gardens, the GWR line runs parallel to the Kennet & Avon Canal. Many of the navvies who helped build the canal were later employed to build the railway; both first envisaged to primarily transport goods. But passengers needed to board somewhere and so a station at Bath was required. The topography of the city centre forced the line to be built on an embankment behind the station building, so the platforms are elevated on the first floor. First-, second- and third-class passengers originally had their own sets of stairs and the platforms had separate 'pens'. Bath Spa opened in 1841 with Brunel designing it in a Jacobean style, although the ground floor windows and fanlights could be Georgian if you really squint. In his book *Britain's 100 Best Railway Stations*, Simon Jenkins declares that even today it looks out of place. Although, of course, it is included in Jenkins' book so cannot be all bad.

ADDRESS Bath Spa, Dorchester Street, BA1 1SU, www.gwr.com/stations-and-destinations/stations/bath-spa TIP Avon Valley Cyclery (www.avonvalleycyclery.co.uk) is located within one of the arches underneath the railway station, providing bikes to the people of Bath since 1979.

9 Bath Stamp & Coin Shop

A shop on a bridge

A sign in the window of Bath Stamp & Coin Shop on Pulteney Bridge informs the countless passers-by of the trade of this establishment: 'We are always interested in buying collections and accumulations of stamps, coins, medals and banknotes. Ancient and modern, British and world, all are potentially of interest. We also buy old letters, tokens and medallions, military cap badges, and gold coins such as sovereigns and Krugerrands.' (If you are not a coin collector – also known as a numismatist – a Krugerrand is the world's first gold bullion coin that was released by South Africa in 1967.)

Shop manager Mike Swindells is the son of Audrey and Harold Swindells, who owned a newsagents on Northumberland Place, where he also sold stamps, which led to him opening Bath Stamp Shop on Pulteney Bridge in 1959. Mike's mother Audrey developed an interest in coins, and his parents' business became the Bath Stamp & Coin Shop in the late 1960s. The pair opened Bath Postal Museum in the basement of their house at 51 Great Pulteney Street in 1977. It later moved to Bath's former post office on Northgate Street before closing in 2023 a few months after the death of Audrey.

Bath Stamp & Coin Shop is located close to the middle of Pulteney Bridge, which has shops on both sides including ones selling antique maps, jewellery, mosaics and flowers. Designed by Robert Adam and built between 1769 and 1774, Pulteney Bridge acts as the gateway from the historic city of Bath to the new Bathwick Estate across the River Avon. Despite being one of Bath's premier landmarks, it is quite possible to walk across the famous span without even realising that you are on a bridge. That was the intention of Adam's unique design: to incorporate the small bridge seamlessly into the streetscape, with pedestrians beckoned into the ever-changing shops along it for the last 250 years.

ADDRESS 12–13 Pulteney Bridge, BA2 4AY, +44 (0)1225 463073 **TIP** Pulteney Bridge is the scene of Inspector Javert's death by suicide in the 2012 film adaptation of *Les Misérables*, with Bath doubling for 19th-century Paris.

10 Batheaston Toll Bridge

Romantically designed
but commercially underpinned

The original charges for crossing Batheaston Toll Bridge on different contraptions and by various means are still displayed on a handwritten sign next to the bridge. At least, they were the prices when the anonymous calligrapher was commissioned. Walking on your own? Ha'pence, please. Crossing with a wheelbarrow? That will be one penny. Riding on horseback? Two pennies. Have a donkey and cart with you? Threepence. A private car cost 6d (that is how pence was written in ye olden days) and seems to have been added on the sign almost as an afterthought. These days, pedestrians and cyclists can cross for free but motorbikes have to pay 50p and cars £1.

Still within living memory, most of Bath's bridges were tolls. Today, Batheaston Toll Bridge is the only one still remaining, thanks to being owned by a private company rather than the local authority. Made of Bath stone, the current structure has been in operation over the River Avon since 1872, connecting Batheaston with Bathampton – and according to who you speak to is named after either place. The toll house – which like the bridge is Grade II-listed – is on the Batheaston side of the bridge next to a mill that has been converted into a hotel that still has a working water wheel.

In recent years, the charges for crossing Batheaston Toll Bridge have increased, and a survey in 2022 found that the bridge is one of the 10 most profitable toll crossings in the UK, falling just behind the Clifton Suspension Bridge. It was said to earn more than £1.3 million annually, not quite at the levels of the Dartford Crossing on the M25, which rakes in more than £200 million each year. Remarkably, the Swinford Bridge that crosses the Thames in Oxfordshire costs car drivers just 5p to cross; cheaper than it was when Batheaston's anonymous calligrapher wrote their handwritten sign all those years ago.

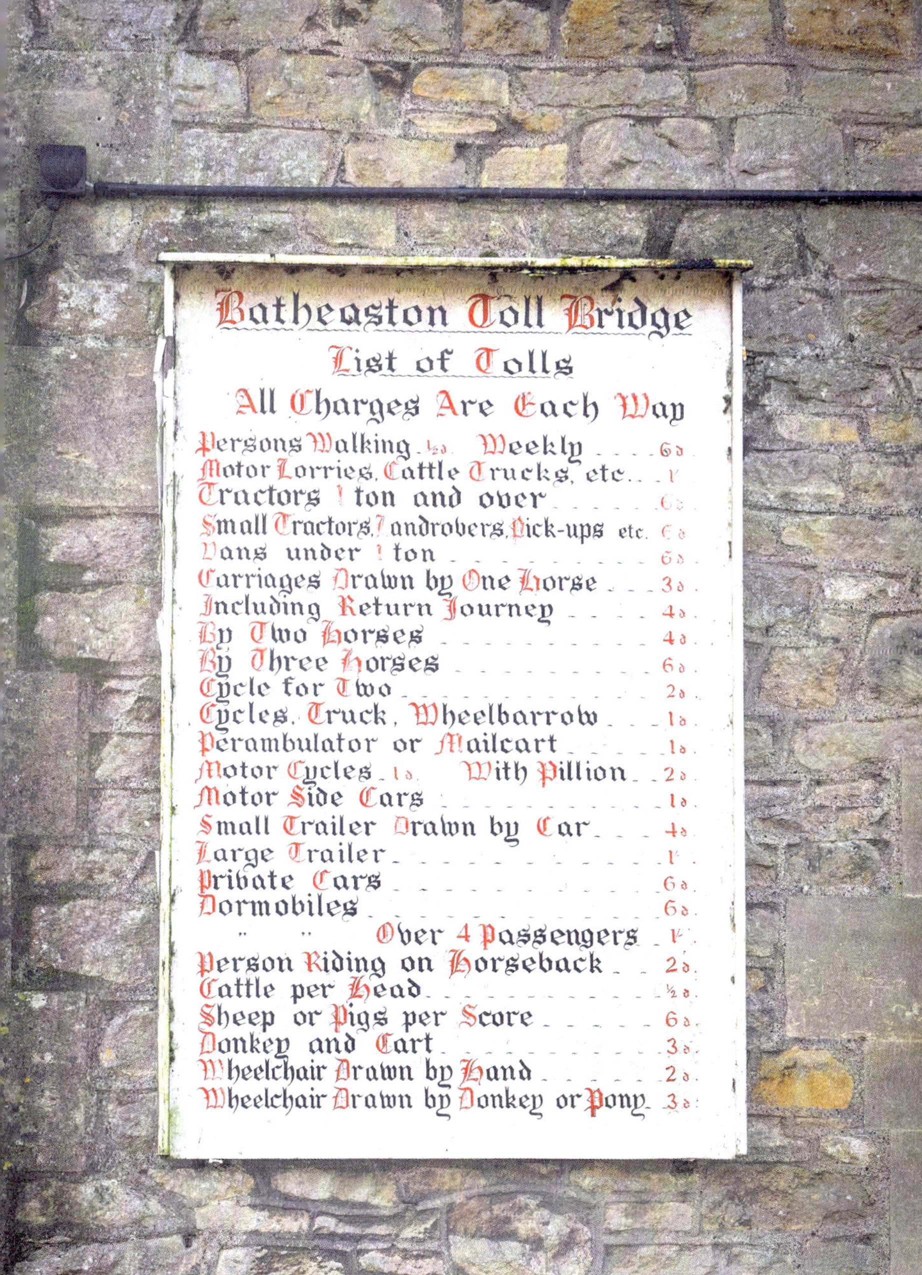

ADDRESS Batheaston Toll Bridge, Toll Bridge Road, BA1 7DE **TIP** Bathampton Meadows close to the bridge is the National Trust's first 'green corridor', linking the city centre to the surrounding countryside and safeguarding the land from future development.

11 Beazer Maze

A petite labyrinth

What's the difference between a maze and a labyrinth? No need to ask ChatGPT; let *111 Places in Bath That You Shouldn't Miss* be your guide. Labyrinths have a single continuous path that leads to the centre and are impossible to get lost in; while mazes have multiple paths that branch off, most of which will not lead to the centre if you take a wrong turn. Mazes most likely derived from labyrinths, the most famous of which is the dark underground labyrinth at Knossos on the Aegean island of Crete in which the Minotaur was imprisoned. Greek mythology is only one place that sees the appearance of a labyrinth, which is thought to have once had a religious meaning as a path to God, ancestors or enlightenment.

So now you know that, you will realise that the Beazer Maze with its unicursal path is in fact a labyrinth. It's named after the Bath-founded construction company who donated the land on which the circuitous contours can be found. The business had originally hoped to build flats here but the land was eventually donated to the city for public use. The maze – sorry, labyrinth – is located next to Bath Rugby's Recreation Ground, where Beazer Ltd founder Cyril Beazer was a former club chairman. He named many of his firm's developments after some of Bath's best rugby players.

The Beazer Maze was designed by diplomat-turned-'labyrinthologist' Randoll Coate in 1984. Two of Coate's other designs can be found in Longleat Safari Park south of the city, where the Marquess of Bath commissioned him to create the Lunar Labyrinth and Sun Maze. His labyrinth in Bath made mostly of paving stones is inspired by Georgian architecture and Isambard Kingdom Brunel's railway designs, and centred on a mosaic that features, among other elements, the Gorgon's head that once looked down at visitors to the Roman baths and the part-man part-bull Minotaur himself.

ADDRESS Beazer Garden, Spring Gardens Road, BA2 1EE TIP After exploring the labyrinth, head to the Italian restaurant next to it, Ponte Vecchio (www.pontevecchiobath.com), located in a converted boat house.

12 Beckford's Tower

'I am not over-fond of resisting temptation'

The eccentric and reclusive William Beckford used to call them 'worldlings', his peers in Georgian society who failed to share his own erudition. He had his tower built for him between 1825 and 1827, and used to ride up here each morning from his home on Lansdown Crescent, accompanied by a pack of spaniels, passing through a grotto-like tunnel. He was then able to enjoy the treasures he had accumulated that he packed into the Greco-Roman tower, which he described as having 'the finest prospect in Europe'.

The Beckford family became extraordinarily wealthy from owning sugar plantations in Jamaica. Huge profits came at the expense of the brutal treatment of enslaved people, which included burning alive the leader of an uprising. Beckford, his father's only legitimate child, had Mozart as a private music tutor. But Beckford was bisexual at a time when sex between men was a capital offence, and a relationship with an 11-year-old boy saw him fleeing into exile in Europe with his wife Margaret. This led to him being ostracised from the society his father so wanted him to be part of.

Beckford's splendid collection of furniture and antiques was first kept at Fonthill Abbey in Wiltshire, which once had a tower 84 metres tall. His tower in Bath is a mere 47 metres tall but stands on one of the highest points in the landscape surrounding the city. The tower and museum reopened in 2024 following a £3.9 million refurbishment project, which also rediscovered the tunnel that Beckford used to pass through on his way to and from his tower. Within the grotto were found clay pipes smoked by the men who built it in the 1820s. Beckford himself would recognise the rich furnishings of the two-bedroom holiday let within the accommodation block at the base of the tower that is now a Landmark Trust property. It is available to stay in for your own retreat away from the 'worldlings'.

ADDRESS Lansdown Road, BA1 9BH, www.beckfordstower.org.uk
TIP Two other nearby towers are Blaine's Tower, also known as Blaine's Folly, constructed for Sir Robert Blaine after he bought Summerhill Park in 1868; and Lansdown Water Tower, which was built in 1925.

13 Blowout Sax

The joy of sax

Look on one wall of Blowout Sax and you will see a framed Guinness World Records certificate. It's for the largest saxophone ensemble ever assembled – 529 musicians – who played on 21 May 2004 in front of the Royal Crescent.

So, for Blowout Sax founder Mark Archer, who helped organise the event in the presence of legendary saxophonist Pee Wee Ellis, what is it about the saxophone? 'It's the sound, man,' he wrote in his report of the record-breaking event. 'That siren sound that can translate a feeling into notes, transmitting those basic emotions of sadness, anger, fear to love, tenderness and the expression of unadulterated joy. It can deliver any feeling. Couple that with the cool look of a saxophone. The additionally super-personality charge. It's like falling in love again with a legitimate lover. And that love affair lasts forever. And it's a personal. With your very own personal sound. The ultimate buzz of self-expression.'

Blowout Sax is the bricks and mortar embodiment of Mark's approach to making learning the saxophone 'quick, easy and maximum fun' with no prior musical knowledge even required. Lessons here run six days a week and each session lasts 45 minutes 'because that's as long as you have puff for'. Mark is a self-taught saxophonist and has distilled his own teaching technique within a book if you can't make it to Bath.

This one is not an official record but Mark calls the unusual building that is the home of Blowout Sax the smallest saxophone school in the world. What was first started in his flat is now located in a Jacobean-style lodge, built between 1835 and 1836 as part of North Parade Bridge. The bridge itself is an extension of North Parade, which was originally called Grand Parade and intended as a summer promenade, with promenades today able to be enjoyed with the backdrop of the siren sound of the saxophone.

ADDRESS South Lodge, North Parade, BA2 4EU, +44 (0)1225 339007, www.blowoutsax.com TIP Bath Music Festival is an annual event of classical music in some of Bath's most beautiful venues (www.bathfestivals.org.uk/bath-music-festival).

14 Bog Island

Spending a penny

Talk to many Bath residents and among the grumbles about traffic and the proliferation of student flats will come a constant moan: the lack of loos. It was all so different, as a patch of land at Terrace Walk is testament to. A shop called Bog Island Convenience Store is named after what this area is called by almost everyone. Now an empty patch of tarmac on which countless coach trippers disembark, it was once surrounded by luxury shops and had the Lower Assembly Rooms on its eastern side, which was the place to see and be seen in Georgian society.

Road widening in the 1930s created this triangular site with land excavated beneath Terrace Walk to create underground public lavatories. Spotlessly clean and immaculately maintained, an always-shining brass handrail led the way down to the men's and women's loos. You could once spend a penny to, um, spend a penny; or pay 6p to have a bath – that payment also getting you a freshly laundered towel and a bar of soap. Opaque blocks in the roof gave a view of feet walking overhead.

When the toilets closed, they had a second wind from the 1970s as a restaurant and private members establishment called the Island Club. The club's metal signage remains to this day – much to the chagrin of the council who unsuccessfully demanded its removal since it had been erected without the requisite planning permission. And then came the subterranean space's third and final act as a nightclub whose owners included former Bath rugby players Roger Spurrell and Peter Heindorff. Affectionately known as Bog Island, the club was a nighttime staple in the 1980s and '90s with one of its main draws a late licence until the early hours of the morning. Many a memorable time was had in this subterranean lair. But all good things have to come to an end, and that signage is all that now remains of one of Bath's most unusual spaces.

ADDRESS Terrace Walk, BA1 1LN TIP It now costs 20p to use Healthmatic-operated public toilets in Bath (www.bathnes.gov.uk/find-public-toilet).

15 Bollards

Bath's 'ring of steel'

Watching a pair of bollards slide apart or together like two dancing Daleks is now a regular sight on roads in the city centre, including York Street and Upper Borough Walls. For their detractors, this is part of 'Fortress Bath': a scheme designed for maximum inconvenience, especially for car drivers. In reality, however, these bollards are aimed at reducing the risk of a terrorist attack as tragically seen in cities across the world. In official parlance, they are 'Hostile Vehicle Mitigation' measures that work in tandem with other features including nigh-on impenetrable street furniture to keep people safe.

One of the locations of the sliding bollards is Cheap Street, which raises a wry chuckle because their installation was anything but cheap. Adding to the expense was the fact that each location required bespoke solutions. Underground pipes carrying electricity, gas and water had to be diverted; and some of the bollards' foundations were constructed to span across the roofs of centuries-old cellars. The scheme's original £2.2 million cost later more than tripled to £7.4 million, and teething problems saw one of the bollards on Cheap Street failing to slide and paramedics even once having to attend a patient on foot when ambulance access was blocked. Later issues saw the sliding bollards having to be operated manually for more than a month due to a problem with the video intercom.

The final bollards as part of the City Centre Security Scheme – also known as the 'ring of steel' – were put in place in 2024 in time for that year's Christmas Market, a period when streets are at their busiest. But it is not Bath's final battle with bollards, as 'liveable neighbourhood' trial schemes introduced in 2022 are made permanent, with more traditional static bollards replacing planters in a number of areas to prevent through-traffic and create more pleasant places to live.

ADDRESS Various locations in the city centre TIP 'Everybody acquainted with Bath may remember the difficulties of crossing Cheap Street,' wrote Jane Austen in *Northanger Abbey*. There were no sliding bollards in her day.

16 Brickfields Park

The clue is in the name

You don't need to be an etymologist to work out the reason behind the name of Brickfields Park. An almost-figure-of-eight-shaped bench made mostly out of bricks is another clue as to this area's industrial origins. Once known as 'the brickyard', it was previously occupied by market gardens, pasture and an orchard. Bath was growing, however, so when Thomas May purchased this rural spot in 1893, he had visions of building houses on the land for the expanding population.

May never realised his vision of any darling buds of housing. Instead, a large clay deposit was revealed just under the topsoil. This was perfect for making not just bricks but also chimneys, flowerpots and pipes. Ever the entrepreneur, May changed tack. His idea of homes was replaced with a brickworks company named after the queen: the Victoria Brick & Tile Works. The land was transformed and coke-fired brick kilns belched out smoke from giant chimneys, including one at the bottom of Lymore Gardens that was 120 feet (37 metres) tall. The business was based here from 1900 to 1942, providing many of the bricks used to build houses during that time in nearby Oldfield Park and Southdown. Clay was dug out by hand until the clay deposits were exhausted and all that remained was a huge crater.

Today, Brickfields Park contains a playground, pump track and Bath's only free full-size basketball court. In recent years, the Your Park charity has chosen this green space to become 'an exemplar park for accessibility for women and girls'. Focusing in particularly on the needs of teenage girls, a round of improvements have included the installation of the five-way swing, and a tree trunk social seating and climbing area; reducing the height of hedges to improve sightlines; and the building of the bespoke brick bench as somewhere to sit as well as harking back to what this place was in its industrial heyday.

ADDRESS King George's Road, BA2 1BJ, www.bathnes.gov.uk/brickfields-park
TIP A parkrun takes place at Brickfields Park at 9am every Saturday morning. The 3-mile (5-kilometre) course starts and finishes in the park and heads along Linear Park as far as the Devonshire Tunnel (www.parkrun.org.uk/brickfieldspark).

17 Café on the Barge

A floating feast

'Do you want a slice of cake?' one customer asked her friend on a recent morning as they were visiting Café on the Barge. There's only one response to a question like that and she soon returned to their bench with a generous portion of carrot cake and a flapjack. Ordering might take a bit of working out for the uninitiated. A couple of steps lead down to a window at ankle level and it is here where you put in your own order for cake, tea, coffee, panini or ice cream – with the latter available for consumption both by humans and by dogs.

Café on the Barge is owned by Heni, who knows all her regulars by name. The location of her business is almost preposterously bucolic and could not be more English if it tried. Previously a busy wharf where barges were loaded with Bath stone for transportation on the Kennet & Avon Canal as far as London, it is now a haven of peace and tranquillity within a village setting only two miles from the city centre. A small bridge just a stone's throw away still has a sign saying it is unable to carry a 'heavy motorcar'. Near the bridge is St Nicholas Church, which has 13th-century origins. Seating space is at a premium on popular days with two picnic tables on a small area of wooden decking and two more the other side of the canal towpath. There are also benches under the trees that offer much-needed shade from the summer sun.

Walk, run or cycle along the canal towpath and you would be forgiven for missing Café on the Barge. But that would be a crying shame as this is one of the most delightful places in Bath for a pit stop. Sit down and enjoy your food and drink accompanied by the faint rustling of the leaves of a weeping willow tree and the chug-chug-chug of passing boats, occasionally interrupted by the tinkling of cyclists' bells as swans and cygnets glide by. Finished your cake? It's time for another slice.

ADDRESS 1896 Tyning Road, Bathampton, BA2 6TQ, +44 (0)7765 703194
TIP Dating from the mid-17th century, the George Inn (www.chefandbrewer.com/pubs/somerset/george-inn) is only a few hundred yards from Café on the Barge and has a beer garden overlooking the canal.

18 Chapel Arts Centre

The best acoustics in Bath

You can enjoy music of all kinds ('except the very loud!') at Chapel Arts Centre, a venue previously known as the Central Club, Window Arts Centre and Invention Studios. Events here range from theatre to dance to comedy and are mostly cabaret-style, with audience members seated at small café tables. It means that nights are unusually intimate, with just 120 people gathered around the tables or up to 200 at a standing gig to enjoy music that is definitely not being turned up to 11.

The small team here pride themselves on running Bath's top alternative arts venue as well as having the best acoustics of any venue in the city. Their function of a community arts centre is specified in their lease and they offer reduced hire rates for community groups, charities, educational organisations and 'anything of a direct community support nature'. But many professionals also pass through their doors, as well as professionals pretending to be other professionals; with regular tribute acts for the likes of David Bowie, Kate Bush and Elton John.

Look above the entrance to Chapel Arts Centre and you will see the words 'St James's Memorial Hall' carved into the Bath stone. This much-loved venue was originally the hall of the former church of St James that used to stand at the top of Southgate Street where the former M&S stands today. The church was one of the buildings hit during the 'Baedeker raids' in 1942 and was eventually demolished in 1957.

Tucked away out of sight but well worth a visit within the basement of the building is Plant Eat Licious (www.planteatlicious.com), a vegan café and restaurant with sustainability at its heart that started off as a food stall during the pandemic. Cristina and her team serve hearty breakfasts, all-day brunches and sharing platters, as well as decadent afternoon teas and the occasional Romanian supper club.

ADDRESS 9 Lower Borough Walls, BA1 1QR, +44 (0)1225 461700, www.chapelarts.org **TIP** The Forum on St James Parade is Bath's largest theatre-style performance venue, hosting regular live music, stand-up comedy and more (www.bathforum.co.uk).

19 The Chapel Forge

Bath's bespoke blacksmiths

It was while he was taking a shortcut home from college that Demian Bellaart first discovered two abandoned chapels in one corner of a cemetery. Demian was studying art at the time and had become increasingly interested in working with metal, soon realising this was the medium he wanted to dedicate himself to. So, he trained in smithery, learning traditional and modern ironwork techniques. But every blacksmith needs their own forge and this was where one of the abandoned chapels would come in useful. No burials have taken place in St Michael's Cemetery for more than a century so the chapels were available for new uses. The octagonal chapel was converted into a workshop, the adjacent building an extra studio, and together they became The Chapel Forge, where raw metal is transformed into beautiful works of art.

Demian and his team of blacksmiths, ironworkers, artists and designers now specialise in creating and restoring gates, balustrades, staircases, railings, handrails, balconies and canopies, as well as creating bespoke sculptural commissions – from weathervanes to window baskets. Being a World Heritage Site, buildings in Bath are regularly in need of restoration, and the craftspeople at The Chapel Forge will employ methods that have remained unchanged for centuries.

'Today, blacksmiths do more than simply hammering,' says Demian on The Chapel Forge website, which also has photos of his well-honed handiwork. 'Part of their business is to visit clients, survey sites, discuss design ideas, provide individual design proposals and make drawings, in addition to making, finishing and installing the work. New methods like computer-aided design, sophisticated welding, fabrication, cutting systems and power hammers have added to the capabilities of modern blacksmiths, but have not compromised the hand skills that lie at the heart of the craft.'

ADDRESS Octagonal Chapel, St Michael's Cemetery, St Michael's Road, Lower Weston, BA1 3BJ, +44 (0)1225 329669, www.thechapelforge.squarespace.com
TIP The Bath Priory hotel just a few hundred yards from St Michael's Cemetery hosts regular events throughout the year, including tours of its award-winning gardens (www.thebathpriory.co.uk).

20 Chelsea Road

A road with community at its heart

'Community really does matter' says a sign in chalk outside one shop on Chelsea Road. It sums up the spirit of this neighbourhood. Start at the bottom of the road with your back to the post office and on a recent evening you could look forward to 'a taste of Peru' supper club at Rooted, which in 2024 featured in a list in *The Times* of where top chefs book for brunch. 'It does get very busy, but it is worth squeezing past the prams and oat milk flat white drinkers,' says Rob Sachdev of Landrace. Talking of top chefs, towards the top of the road is a gastronomic experience from James Wilkins with only six seats. Wilks was a Michelin-starred restaurant in Bristol before moving to Bath in 2023. Want something less fancy? Pizzarella serves not just pizza but also fish and chips and kebabs.

Community Matters is in fact the name of a charity shop that supports a different Bath charity each year. On the other side of the road is another charity shop, HUGS, with a window display – dolls house, silver cutlery and a wedding dress – befitting of some of the finest antiques shops in town. All of the profits here go towards cancer services at the nearby RUH Hospital. As other shops come and go, a stalwart on Chelsea Road for decades has been Homecharmer ironmongery and hardware. If you ask nicely, they might even be able to sell you fork handles.

Next to Mai Thai restaurant is Una, selling jewellery, prints, art and much more, promising to be 'handmade, local, unique'. And opposite Mai Thai is Paprika selling gifts, clothing and accessories. Chelsea Road Deli is both a shop and a café while 8e serves brunch from Friday to Monday; and sandwiches, granola and baked goods from Tuesday to Thursday. Cadence is an aptly named bike shop at the top of the road, and if you have been going for a King of the Mountain segment on Strava, reward yourself with a pint at the New Crown Inn. Walking and cycling will hopefully soon both get safer on Chelsea Road, which is likely to be located within Bath's first Liveable Neighbourhood.

ADDRESS BA1 3PP **TIP** At the top of Chelsea Road, with its main entrance on Upper Bristol Road, is Locksbrook Cemetery. Closed for new burials for more than 80 years, nature is now largely taking over, creating a wildlife haven within the city.

21 Claverton Pumping Station

Georgian green engineering

Canals can be thanked for much of Bath's industrial prosperity, allowing goods to be transported across the country. They were soon overtaken by road and rail but the waterways still form a central feature of much of the city's landscape. A few miles from the city centre is the original pump that kept the Kennet & Avon Canal topped up, and it remains in complete working order despite having started life in 1813, the same year *Pride and Prejudice* was published.

A pump was needed here because of leaks, with boats often unable to pass through this section of the canal because of a lack of water. Claverton Pumping Station uses the power of the River Avon to drive a waterwheel that lifts water up 48 feet (15 metres) into the canal. It may have been the start of the steam era but this pump burns no fuel and creates no waste. It is an exemplar piece of environmentally friendly green technology from the Georgian Regency period.

In an engineering version of the 'Dem Bones' song where the thigh bone's connected to the hip bone, the river runs into the waterwheel and turns it, with the wheel then rotating five times a minute, turning a big gear, that turns a smaller gear, which moves two beams and powers the pump. Two tonnes of water a second are needed to drive the waterwheel.

The Canal & River Trust own the pumphouse building but it is a dedicated group of volunteers who run and manage it. One of their regular jobs is having to clean out silt following a flood, now happening with increased regularity, with marks on the wall from some of the highest river levels over the last 200 years. On their twice-monthly open days, the pumphouse is always open but there is no guarantee that the pump will be working. 'Running of the pump is subject to river conditions, ageing machinery and ageing volunteers,' say the team keeping this engineering masterpiece in working order.

ADDRESS Ferry Lane, Claverton, BA2 7BH, +44 (0)1225 483001, www.claverton.org TIP An ornate chimney next to the canal in Widcombe is all that remains of an old pumping station that once stood here.

22 Coffee in Colonna

The most special speciality coffee

Half a dozen trophies in the front window of Colonna & Small's belong to Maxwell Colonna-Dashwood, the founder of this café and its sister roastery. He is rarely behind the bar these days but the trophies prove that he sure knows what he is doing. The biggest trophy is from when Maxwell won the UK Barista Championships in 2012, positioned next to two fifth-placed finishes at the World Championships held in Rimini in Italy in 2014 and Seattle in the USA in 2015. Maxwell has also literally written the book on coffee, *The Business of Specialty Coffee*, which you can buy alongside an assortment of paraphernalia to upgrade your home set-up.

When you get a Colonna coffee, you know it's going to be one of the best coffees you've ever tasted. It damn well better be if you decide to spend £19 on one filter. For almost the price of a two-course lunch next door in Corkage, this drink is on the 'freezer reserve menu', all of which are kept individually dosed and vacuum sealed. When a customer orders one, the coffee is ground straight from frozen 'for peak flavour clarity'. This menu on a recent visit featured options from Colombia, Panama and Peru. The most expensive was an Esmeralda Special Gesha from 2023, described as 'elegant with a silky texture. Intense florals, crisp citrus acidity and a long sweet finish'.

For a typical order that won't break the bank, there are three choices of espresso beans and three choices of filter beans, costing from £3.35 for a takeaway. There is also a lungo that sits in between espresso and filter. The baristas working behind the bar will happily talk you through the choices of coffee available and highly recommend that you don't add sugar. What is not frowned upon is a pastry or sweet treat to accompany your coffee. Try a slice of the lemon and blueberry cake if you can, as perfectly balanced as the award-winning drinks.

ADDRESS 6 Chapel Row, BA1 1HT, +44 (0)7766 808067, www.colonnacoffee.com/pages/colonna-smalls-bath TIP Just around the corner from Colonna & Small's is No. 11 Espresso Bar on Princes Street, which has an all-vegan menu of cakes, brownies and cookies (@no11espressobar).

23 The Coeur de Lion

Bath's smallest pub

When the Coeur de Lion was threatened with closure in the 1980s, there was an uproar. Even Bath MP Chris Patten, who later became the last governor of Hong Kong, got involved and plans to turn it into a shop were rejected. The irony is that it was Devenish Brewery that had planned to get rid of the pub and it is Devenish whose name remains in the Coeur de Lion's splendid stained-glass windows.

Abbey Ales are the current custodians of Bath's smallest pub, which has had the same name since 1880 but whose etymology has been lost in the mists of time, having also previously been called Marchants Court and the Avondale Stores. The Abbey Ales brewery also owns the Star Inn on the Paragon, whose 18th-century bar fittings and wooden benches mean it is listed on the UK's national inventory of heritage pubs; and the Assembly Inn on Alfred Street, which has underground comedy club Jesters in its basement.

There is space for only around 20 people to sit on the ground floor of the Coeur de Lion in a room that is smaller than some other pubs' snugs. Hops hang from the ceiling and a framed Bath Rugby shirt from the Powergen Cup Final of 2005 is on one side of the bar. A steep flight of stairs leads to a first-floor room that is even smaller.

On a recent visit soundtracked to '90s classics from Take That and the Backstreet Boys on the stereo, there were three ales on tap: Bellringer and Bath Pale Ale from Abbey Ales, and Timothy Taylor's Landlord. The first known landlord here was a woodcarver called William Batt, who gained a licence to sell beer at number 4 Northumberland Place in around 1860 before the pub was moved over the road in 1886 to where it remains. One visitor to the Coeur de Lion sat on a chair with a metal plaque marking that this was 'Bullshit Corner'. He began to regale his companion with tall tales about Bath's smallest pub.

ADDRESS 17 Northumberland Place, BA1 5AR, +44 (0)1225 463568, www.abbeyinnsbath.co.uk/#coeur-de-lion-pub-bath **TIP** Just a few doors from the Coeur de Lion is Coffever, a café and coffee roasters that was founded in Hong Kong before moving to Bath (www.coffever.co.uk).

24 Cranes

A reminder of Bath's industrial revolution

Giant dockside and heavy-duty cranes made in Bath were once exported to all corners of the globe. Find a crane still standing today and the chances are that on it will be the badge of Stothert & Pitt. Once known as 'crane makers to the world', they employed thousands of people between 1855 and 1989. What was previously their works on Lower Bristol Road retains its name of Newark Works and is now part of the Bath Quays regeneration area with industrial-style workspaces.

Close to Mokoko café at Newark Works is a six-ton hand-operated crane believed to be the oldest known surviving crane constructed by Stothert & Pitt. Built around 1864, it functioned as a stone quarry crane at Box in Wiltshire and, when its working life was over, spent some years in a garden before being restored and put in place back in Bath where it had been built.

Another original Stothert & Pitt crane is at the end of Victoria Bridge Road in what was previously the firm's Victoria Works and a derelict site until it was turned into a housing development. This one was manufactured around 1904 and is one of the last remaining rail-mounted self-propelled steam cranes built by the company. Former mayor of Bath and industrial historian, Bryan Chalker, was instrumental in the restoration of the crane, which now sits painted in grey and red on a small section of track.

A third surviving crane pre-dating the foundation of Stothert & Pitt can be found close to the Dundas Aqueduct. It is believed that this crane was built by Acramans of Bristol during the early 1830s and first handled cargo at Broad Quay Street, moving to its current location in 1894 to replace a wooden crane. Its job was to lift cargo and blocks of stone on and off boats, with a surviving Georgian toll house near the place where tolls were paid – calculated by multiplying tonnes of cargo by the distance travelled.

ADDRESS Newark Works, 2 Foundry Lane, BA2 3DZ; 13 Victoria Bridge Road, BA2 3EH; Dundas Aqueduct, Brassknocker Basin, Monkton Combe, BA2 7JD
TIP The name Stothert & Pitt lives on in both a rugby club and a bowls club.

25 Delia's Grotto

An 18th-century scandal

Bath has a particular propensity for follies – those architectural extravagances popular during the 18th and 19th centuries that serve no specific purpose other than for aesthetic pleasure. There are temples, towers and even a castle.

Hidden away in the riverside garden of a Greek restaurant, there is a folly with a scandalous history that even features in a poem, the first two verses of which go: 'Uncouth is this moss cover'd grotto of stone / And damp is the shade of this dew dripping tree; / Yet I this rude grotto with rapture will own; / And willow thy damps are refreshing to me. / For this is the grotto where Delia reclin'd / As late I in secret her confidence sought; / And this is the tree kept her safe from the wind, / As blushing she heard the grave lesson I taught.'

Those stanzas were written by Irish playwright Richard Sheridan who romantically pursued Elizabeth Linley, a talented singer and notable beauty. Made out of limestone in the early 18th century, the reason behind the name Delia's Grotto has been lost in time.

It is also unknown where this archway was originally located but it is believed to have once been within Harrison's Walks, a former pleasure ground. What is known is that the grotto played a central role in the courtship of Richard and Elizabeth, with a story varying with who you hear it from – as Richard either leaving poems for Elizabeth at the grotto or the pair meeting in secret there away from prying eyes. In 1772, the pair eloped (as remembered by a plaque on the side of the former Linley family home at 11 Royal Crescent) and were married in a village near Calais; a marriage that neither of their families accepted as legal. Fighting not one but two duels over his beloved, Richard won the first but was badly wounded in the second, saved – as another story goes – by one sword-thrust stopped by a miniature of Elizabeth.

ADDRESS In the garden of Opa, 14 North Parade, BA2 4AJ TIP Find another similar-sized folly to Delia's Grotto in front of Henrietta Court on Bathwick Street, which was originally part of an entrance to architect John Pinch the Younger's building yard.

26 Divine Savages

Injecting splashes of wonder

The late 18th-century terraced houses of Margaret's Buildings are now home to Bath's most eclectic collection of shops. This isn't the place you can pop to in your pyjamas to get a pint of milk. But talking of pyjamas, the Divine Savages store may specialise in wallpaper but it also sells luxury loungewear; its pyjamas, robes and even an eye mask all made from satin. So stroll along Margaret's Buildings (thought to be named after a former countess of Bath) in your luxury loungewear to find artwork, skincare, books, clothes, furniture and even Japanese toys from the basement of Komorebi at number 7.

Divine Savages is run by husband and husband team Jamie Watkins and Tom Kennedy, who promise 'a rebellious approach to design'. Some of that design has been influenced by their dearly departed cat, Ripley, who became the unlikely muse for one of their most popular collections: Cat-titude. 'Her regal demeanour and undeniable sass perfectly embody the Divine Savages spirit,' say Tom and Jamie. 'Confident, characterful and completely unapologetic.'

Tom began drafting wallpaper designs in 2017 when the pair lived in London and were not able to find wallpapers to match their own unique style. Their first showroom and shop opened in Bath six years later promising 'a maximalist's dream' with wallpaper, fabrics, cushions, lampshades and gifts.

'Forget mass-produced, boring and uninspiring design,' add Tom and Jamie. 'Our mission here at Divine Savages is to deliver you stunning wallpapers and fabrics, gorgeous home accessories, limited edition art prints and beautiful gifts. With eye-catching and eclectic creations that add personality, glamour and style to any interior, our collections bring a wild reworking of the traditional. Fusing both classic and modern, each of our designs offer you the chance to turn every room into a living masterpiece.'

ADDRESS 5 Margaret's Buildings, BA1 2LP, +44 (0)1225 532340, www.divinesavages.com TIP Match your new wallpaper to furniture, lighting, ceramics and decorative objects from the Hessian Collective, run by the family team of Louise, Oliver, Scarlett and India Hessian (www.hessiancollective.com).

27 Dr Oliver

Inventor of a biscuity bastion of Britishness

There aren't many biscuits that have their own preservation society. But there aren't many biscuits like the Bath Oliver, a cracker-like creation invented by Dr William Oliver that is often eaten with cheese and accompanied by a glass of fortifying liquor. When production was halted in 2020, there was an outcry. *The Daily Telegraph* alled the news 'a national tragedy' and Conservative Party grandee Jacob Rees-Mogg, former MP for North East Somerset (the constituency neighbouring Bath), mourned the death of the 'best British biscuit'. Food writer Felicity Cloake called the Bath Oliver the 'salty yin to the Rich Tea's yang'. But all was not lost, and manufacturer Jacob's continued production, with fans once again stocking up their store cupboards.

Oliver was born in Cornwall in 1695 and trained as a doctor, originally practising in Plymouth before moving to Bath, becoming medical adviser to Alexander Pope, and friends with Beau Nash and Ralph Allen. Described as a domineering personality, he achieved serious financial success, which enabled him to move with his family into a newly built house designed by John Wood on Queen Square. As well as his private practice, he was also one of the founders of the General Hospital, which opened in 1742. He invented his eponymous hard and dry cracker in 1750, believing that it would be a digestive aid for his wealthy patients, many of whom had come to Bath's thermal waters for treatment of gout. The recipe was later passed to his coachman, a Mr Atkins, along with a sack of flour and £100, and continued to be produced in huge quantities from a factory in the city, for many years stamped with Oliver's face.

The Britishness of the biscuit was such that it was in a Bath Oliver tin that the Crown Jewels were hidden underground beneath Windsor Castle for the duration of World War II. Their own preservation was thus secured forevermore.

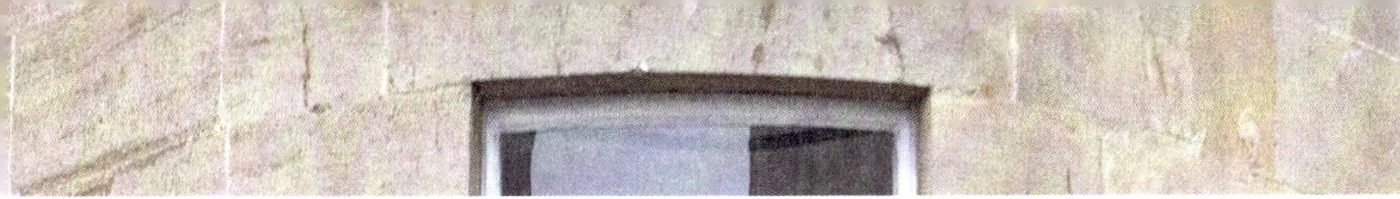

ADDRESS Dr Oliver's plaque is above 9 Green Street, BA1 2JY TIP Find a recipe for the Bath Oliver on the website of the Bath Oliver Preservation Society (www.batholiver.com).

28 Eastgate

The last survivor of the medieval city gates

To look down at Eastgate from above is to see how the street level of Bath has risen over time to avoid flooding from the River Avon. Eastgate is the only surviving gate from the medieval wall that once surrounded Bath. The other gates and almost the entirety of the wall have been demolished over the years in order to make way for Bath's 18th-century transformation. But the wall and gates do live on in a few place names, and a small section of the wall still remains on Upper Borough Walls. Talking of place names, do you see that small passageway running through the Eastgate? That is Boat Stall Lane, which heads down from here to the river. It comes out near the weir in front of Pulteney Bridge at an area previously known as Boat Stall Quay, where there was a ferry to a mill and Bathwick on the other side.

Because it was connected to a ferry rather than a road, Eastgate was never one of the busiest thoroughfares in and out of the medieval city. Its narrowness is a further clue but its significance remains as a survivor while virtually everything around it changed beyond all recognition. Oh, to be a fly on the wall (yes, pun intended) in the meetings of the all-powerful Bath Corporation, who between 1754 and 1776 ordered the demolition of the city's north, west and south gates. The Bath we know of today would not have been created without their decisions that rendered the medieval streetscape almost invisible during the resultant building boom.

And so we return to the Eastgate, resolutely remaining among bins, beer barrels, parked cars and the occasional smoker. Its original name may not be marked on some maps any more, but it is still possible to follow the old route of Boat Stall Lane from Grand Parade to Orange Grove, just a few metres higher now than when it once led through one of the four gateways into the medieval city.

ADDRESS To the side of Bath Guildhall Market, 33 High Street, BA2 4AW (what3words: wallet.insist.heavy) TIP The River Avon is tautology. The Celtic word for river is 'afon', with various rivers across the UK named Avon, literally meaning River River.

29 Elf & Fairy Foray

A real-life fairytale in the woods

Fifteen elf and fairy folk live among the greenery in Long Wood. They are not easy to locate but look closely and you will find the front doors of their miniature homes. It helps if you are a little person too because the doors are positioned at the base of trees. If you are a bit bigger, crouch down to get the best view. It's okay, you won't embarrass yourself: Ring doorbells have yet to cross over from the human world to fairytales. Each tiny door has its own number and a nearby sign tells you the names of a few of the whimsical residents, including North Pepperfly at number 12 and Bracken Elfy at number 3.

The Elf & Fairy Foray at Long Wood – also known as Rainbow Wood because of its arc shape – has play equipment made out of the natural environment, created in consultation with children at Combe Down School. If you have already found the doors, let off steam on the rope swing, stepping logs and see-saw, or build your own den. At the woodland play area's opening, a National Trust spokesperson said they hoped it would 're-kindle the love of the great outdoors by bringing communities together to explore, discover and have fun in our wonderful natural settings'. And if searching for doors is not for you, use your phone's GPS to go geocaching to find hidden treasure (www.geocaching.com/play).

Long Wood is part of the family discovery trail along the National Trust-owned Bath Skyline to the south-east of the city. It is six miles in total: easy if you have sprouted fairy wings. Or walk on your own two feet along the full length of Bath Skyline, whose footpaths are clearly marked on ground level. This stretch of Bath Skyline encompasses Claverton Down, a plateau above the steep slopes of Bathwick. Look out for cattle and sheep grazing at Rainbow Wood Farm, young lambs playing in the fields, and perhaps even your new elf and fairy friends.

ADDRESS Long Wood, off Claverton Down Road, BA2 7AU, www.nationaltrust.org.uk/bath-skyline **TIP** A short walk from Long Wood is Team Bath's Sports Training Village, whose facilities include the UK's only bobsleigh and skeleton push-start track, where 2026 Winter Olympics gold medallists Matt Weston and Tabby Stoecker both train.

30 First King of All England

Edgar the Peaceful was crowned in Bath in 973

When Charles III was crowned king in 2023, the service was broadcast live to people watching in Bath Abbey. Just beneath their feet, many of the traditions of the ceremony happening in Westminster Abbey had taken place for the first time more than 1,000 years before. Because it was in Bath where the coronation of Edgar took place and the man known as 'the first king of all England' (his queen, Aelfthryth, also became the first consort to be crowned Queen of England) would undoubtedly recognise elements of his coronation in the one that took place a millennium later.

Bath was likely chosen as the location for the coronation because of its connections to both Wessex and Mercia, being on the border of these two powerful kingdoms. Edgar's coronation unified them and also Northumbria. Edgar's important day became the template for all subsequent monarchs. One significant difference, however, other than the big day moving to London, was that Edgar's coronation took place in the 14th year of his reign as the crowning glory of his tenure, rather than at the beginning of a monarch's ascendancy, which is now customary.

The reason why the modern coronation shares so much with Edgar's is that the service compiled by Dunstan – the Archbishop of Canterbury and a close personal adviser to the king who later became a saint – was dutifully recorded for posterity. Edgar's anointing with oil invoked the Old Testament anointing of King Solomon by Zadok the priest; just one of many elements of the coronation that were carefully choreographed.

The King Edgar Window in Bath Abbey shows in glorious colour what his coronation might have looked like if we were there to see it happen on Whitsunday 973. Younger visitors to Bath Abbey today can dress up as King Edgar to hold their own ceremony, their grown-ups no doubt hoping the children share some of Edgar's famous peacefulness.

ADDRESS Bath Abbey, BA1 1LT, +44 (0)1225 422462, www.bathabbey.org
TIP A stone on the floor of Bath Abbey commemorates the visit of Queen Elizabeth II in 1973 for a service to mark 1,000 years since Edgar's coronation.

31 Freshford Pill Box

A trace of wartime fortifications

An infantry training manual from 1941 shares nine operational procedures for soldiers in a pill box. No. 1: 'The concrete pill box is a great aid to defence if intelligently used. It may also become a death trap.' No. 4b: 'Temporary cover from view, shell fire and aerial bombing may be sought inside the pill box but beware that the enemy is not creeping towards you under covering fire while you are hiding inside.'

The surviving pill boxes near Bath are part of Stop Line Green, a semi-circular line of fortifications also known as the Bristol Outer Defences, which was hastily built from June 1940 due to the imminent threat of a German invasion in World War II. If the German army had got this far across the country, British troops would have been engaged in a desperate rearguard action against attack from the east, with the last-ditch defence of Bristol necessary to keep its port open for evacuation or for resupplies and reinforcements.

The menacing threat of German tanks needed to be immediately halted. To help in this mission, Stop Line Green and others like it utilised existing tank-stopping obstacles such as rivers, railway cuttings and canals. Made out of steel reinforced concrete and with walls up to 50 inches (1.27 metres) thick, pill boxes were positioned at intervals along the line, including one in Freshford next to the natural defence of the River Frome.

A torch, wellies and binoculars are 'essential equipment' when on the look out for pill boxes, according to Major Martin Green in his book *Stop Line Green*. Back in 1940, pill boxes would have been 'large, obvious and easy targets' for the Germans, says Green. Today, they are easier to find in the winter with less vegetation. Duck down and squeeze inside the entrance to this one and peer through the six firing ports that give a 360-degree vantage point. What would you do if you saw a Panzer tank on the horizon?

ADDRESS West of Ilford Lane, Freshford (what3words: enhancement.supper.kick)
TIP Colourful artwork on platform 2 of Freshford station is by Emma Douglas in memory of her son, Cato (www.emmadouglas.com).

32 Garden of Remembrance

A place for quiet contemplation

Sit for a while on the benches surrounding the Memorial Garden in Henrietta Park and you will hear the soothing sound of a small fountain spouting a dancing jet of foamy water into a rectangular pond. Casting a shadow from one side is a tall sycamore tree. Casting its own shadow nearer to the pond is a metal sundial on a stone plinth. Look above your head and you might spot a squirrel darting along the trellis or pergola, on top of which are the intertwined branches of an elderberry bush. Other trees in the park include some of the finest in Bath, with different varieties originating from across the world.

The Garden of Remembrance, to the west of the park off Henrietta Road, was opened in 1936, 'dedicated in honour of King George the Fifth by the city of Bath' according to a plaque by its entrance. The garden may have been originally opened as a memorial to a monarch but on more than a dozen benches are reminders to many other people, with their own small plaques commemorating a number of former users of this park.

In recent years, the space has been redesigned as a sensory garden with particular emphasis on providing an experience for people with visual impairments, with Braille descriptions and vivid blocks of colour.

Before it became Henrietta Park, this land was known as Bathwick Meadows. It was officially opened on 22 June 1897 to celebrate the Diamond Jubilee of Queen Victoria, having been given to the city by Captain Francis William Forester of the Third King's Own Hussars, the owner of the Bathwick Estate, who stipulated that it should always remain a green space. The seven-acre park is owned by the council but has a committed Friends of Henrietta Park (FoHP) group who organise regular litter picking and gardening sessions. In 2020, the pond was emptied and cleaned by the FoHP for the first time in living memory, with the fire brigade helping to refill the water.

ADDRESS Henrietta Park, BA2 6LY, www.bathnes.gov.uk/henrietta-park
TIP On Henrietta Street are two entrances to the former Laura Chapel, where Jane Austen is believed to have been a worshipper.

33 The Georgian Garden

A recreation from when grass was the future

If you think it's unfair that the front of the houses on The Circus get all the attention, then you're in luck because hidden behind one of these astonishing homes is a time-warp back garden. It was in 1985 that work began on recreating a Georgian-style garden here that would replace an existing garden that was mainly Victorian. There was a key problem, however, when it came to designing the plot: there were no illustrations or written descriptions of what it looked like when the house was completed by 1761. That was all right though, as archaeological excavations revealed three distinct garden plans that pre-dated later alterations.

Today's garden attempts to 'recreate the mood of a small town garden from the period'. Don't expect much flamboyance but do walk along the original routes of the paths from that first garden. The beds are also located exactly as they were from around 1770, but the species and location of plants are all based on the best guesswork possible. In a Georgian garden, there would not have been any grass as the mechanical lawn mower had yet to be invented.

The Georgian Garden is part of 4 The Circus, featured in the 2025 BBC 2 documentary *Empire*, presented by historian and *Celebrity Traitors* star David Olusoga. It was revealed that when the house was built, its first resident was James Plunkett, whose family made their fortune owning enslaved people and sugar plantations on Jamaica. His neighbour next door at number 5 was Lawrence Dundas, from another slave-owning family with plantations in Grenada and Dominica. Just two examples of how much of Bath's wealth flowed from the horrors of the transatlantic trade in enslaved Africans. And then there was Robert Clive at number 11, also known as Clive of India, whose own unimaginable riches came from the appalling treatment of millions of people in the Indian subcontinent.

ADDRESS 4 The Circus, BA1 2EW, www.bathnes.gov.uk/georgian-garden TIP Bath's Fashion Museum is due to reopen in 2030 in the former post office on the corner of New Bond Street and Broad Street, featuring 100,000 objects and new communal public spaces (www.fashionmuseum.co.uk).

34 The Gravel Walk

Bath's first bypass

This favourite thoroughfare of Jane Austen – where Anne Elliot and Captain Frederick Wentworth meet in *Persuasion* – can also lay claim to being Bath's first bypass. It was known as Lovers Lane in Austen's time, and Anne and Frederick Wentworth opening their hearts to one another is one of the most romantic scenes in all of Austen's novels. The 2022 Netflix adaptation filmed scenes on the Gravel Walk, which has remained more or less unchanged since first laid out in 1771.

Writing in *Persuasion*, Austen called the path 'the comparatively quiet and retired gravel walk, where the power of conversation would make the present hour a blessing indeed, and prepare it for all the immortality which the happiest recollections of their own future lives could bestow'. Now forming part of Royal Victoria Park, the Gravel Walk was built to provide a new pedestrian path away from the busier roads nearby and still serves its original purpose; bicycles now more prevalent than sedan chairs.

The Gravel Walk was built as a bypass to link the Royal Crescent with Queen Square, and it provides views of the rear façades of Brock Street and the Circus. These vantage points provide an interesting comparison to their frontages, with a key principle in classical architecture the differences between a building's front and rear. While the front was treated reverentially, backs were a private matter and it was up to the owners to do whatever they wished with them. Just take a look at the rear of the Royal Crescent for the best example of the sharp contrasts between front and back.

Despite Bath's close association with Austen to this day, she was largely ambivalent about the city. She spent five mostly unhappy years here and was pleased to move away in 1806. To mark her 250th birthday in 2025, an exhibition was held named after how she once described Bath: 'The Most Tiresome Place in the World'.

ADDRESS Gravel Walk, BA1 2NN TIP Across Royal Avenue from Gravel Walk is the Victoria Falls crazy golf course (www.exceltennisbath.co.uk/adventuregolf).

35 Green Park Station

The end of the line

Green Park is a thriving platform for creativity. Think music workshops, picture framing, a pizzeria and an event space. There are also market stalls selling everything from cutlery to quinoa. The markets take place beneath a magnificent 65-foot (20-metre) high vaulted glazed roof with a focus on food on Fridays, and a huge variety of local produce at the Saturday farmers' market. Then there is Bath Contemporary Artists' Fair on the second Sunday of every month, independent makers at Bath Independent Market on the third Sunday, and vintage wares and antiques every fourth Sunday.

Green Park used to be a terminus of the Midland Railway, one of the largest railway companies of the Victorian and Edwardian eras. It opened in 1870 as Queen Square (only becoming Green Park under British Railways in 1954) with the buildings designed in Georgian style by architect John Holloway Sanders. This was the end of the line for trains to and from Bournemouth, with the station particularly busy in the summer months for trips to the seaside. Unlike Bath Spa, however, trains no longer run in and out of Green Park. The last locomotives left this station still in the age of steam, in 1966, before the nationwide cuts to branch lines by Dr Beeching.

The closure of Green Park might have been a pain for train passengers but it was eventually to be a success for cyclists. The extremely popular Bristol&Bath Railway Path now uses the line between the two cities on a 13-mile traffic-free route. When construction started in 1979, this became the very first section of the National Cycle Network. Look out for the remains of other former stations, including Mangotsfield. There are also artworks along the route, including a sculpture of a Roman soldier created by artist Gordon Young in 1992, marking the spot where the former railway line intersects an old Roman road.

ADDRESS Green Park Road, BA1 1JB, www.greenparkstation.co.uk
TIP Green Park Brasserie hosts regular live music in the station's former ticket hall (www.greenparkbrasserie.com).

36 Haile Selassie's Home

An emperor in exile

His Imperial Majesty, Emperor of Ethiopia, King of Kings and Conquering Lion of the Tribe of Judah. He has been described as the 'conscience of the world', the globe's 'greatest prophet' and the 'father of Africa'. Who was this man? Haile Selassie, believed by many Rastafarians to be the second coming of Christ. Selassie – whose pre-coronation name, Ras Tafari, gives the movement its name – lived in Bath between 1936 and 1940 after being forced to go into exile following Italy's invasion of Ethiopia. From his temporary West Country home, Selassie campaigned against Italian dictator Benito Mussolini and became a worldwide symbol against fascism while still walking his dog around Bath.

Selassie settled in Bath after first visiting for the city's fabled healing waters to treat mustard gas burns on his hands and arms. And it was where he stayed after purchasing a property in Newbridge close to the Royal United Hospital. Ethiopia's last emperor was by no means the only resident of Fairfield House, with his extended family, servants, government ministers and priests all moving in with him. 'It was a big entourage that lived in Bath, so they were very noticeable,' said University of the West of England professor Shawn Naphtali Sobers on a programme for the BBC World Service in 2024, saying the Ethiopians may have been recognisable but they became 'engrained' in the community.

When Selassie left Bath to return to Ethiopia, he was so grateful to the people of Bath for sheltering him during his exile that he donated Fairfield House to the city for use as a home for the elderly. That remains its function today, as well as being a 'meeting point between different cultures, traditions and interest groups with immense healing power'. Selassie always remembered his time in Bath, naming a building in the capital Addis Ababa after his temporary home.

ADDRESS Fairfield House, 2 Kelston Road, BA1 3QJ, +44 (0)1225 464165, www.fairfieldhousebath.co.uk **TIP** Blatain Gueta Herouy, one of Haile Selassie's servants, is buried in Locksbrook Cemetery. His grave is often wrapped in the green, yellow and red flag of Ethiopia.

37 Hand Fountain

Palm prints of the stars

In front of Grauman's Chinese Theatre on Hollywood Boulevard in Los Angeles, there is the Forecourt of the Stars. In front of the Palais des Festivals in Cannes, there is the Allée des Stars. Some of the biggest names in global cinema have their handprints and even footprints on display at these two locations, quite literally cementing themselves in history.

Bath's version is slightly more subtle. There is no Hollywood razzmatazz here. No gobsmackingly gaudy celebration of celebrity. The handprints remain on the sloping edge of what was originally a fountain erected in 1990. Around the fountain now filled with plants rather than water are the left and right palm prints of 16 prominent people who have played at the nearby Theatre Royal. No need for autograph hunting here either as their signatures accompany their handprints, alongside their names just in case you can't make out who they are from the scribbles.

In alphabetical order, the featured thespians are Lionel Blair, Richard Briers, Joan Collins, Pauline Collins, Paul Eddington, Frank Finlay, Edward Fox, Susan Hampshire, Nigel Hawthorne, Michael Hordern, Derek Jacobi, Penelope Keith, Maureen Lipman, Hayley Mills, Juliet Mills and Peter Ustinov.

Among a myriad of honours are knighthoods and damehoods, and awards too numerous to mention. A selection of some of their plaudits are Derek Jacobi being one of the founding members of the National Theatre; Hayley Mills playing the original dual role of teenage twins in *The Parent Trap* in 1961, which was remade with Lindsay Lohan in 1998; Peter Ustinov winning two Oscars including his best-known role as Batiatus in *Spartacus*; and Susan Hampshire being a three-time Emmy winner. Joan Collins is the only person on the Hand Fountain to also have been awarded a star on the Hollywood Walk of Fame. But that's small fry compared to this small fountain in Bath.

ADDRESS Seven Dials Court, BA1 1EN TIP The Theatre Royal's Ustinov Studio on Monmouth Street features in-house productions and small-scale touring theatre, comedy, music and dance (www.theatreroyal.org.uk/ustinov).

38 Ha'penny Bridge

A former toll bridge with a tragic tale

There's not much you can get these days for a ha'penny. In fact, you can get nothing at all as the half penny coin was withdrawn from circulation in the UK in 1984 after it became more expensive to produce than its face value. Some families kept the coins to use for games involving friendly betting at Christmas but the vast majority were melted down for other currency. The ha'penny (or half penny or half-penny; all three are interchangeable) lives on in Bath at the Halfpenny Bridge, a name more commonly given to Widcombe Footbridge because the toll to cross was once a ha'penny. The first bridge connecting Widcombe to the city was built here over the River Avon in 1863, accompanied by a toll house.

Tragically, eight people were killed and many more injured on the morning of 6 June 1877 when the first footbridge collapsed. Hundreds of excited visitors had arrived at Bath Spa railway station on their way to the centenary Bath & West Show. They were waiting to pay the toll on the southern side of the span when the wooden structure broke in two, falling into the water below. *The New York Times*, no less, covered the disaster, reporting that 'the bridge snapped in the centre and the two ends were wrenched clear from the sides. The whole mass, with the people, was plunged into the middle of the stream, which was about seven feet [two metres] deep. Boats from the shore were immediately at work rescuing the living and searching for the dead.'

After the disaster, a replacement bridge was built using a more stable steel box girder structure on the same piers as the earlier bridge. Walk below the bridge on the river footpath and on a buttress on the Widcombe side, you will be able to see more than a dozen engraved dates between 1866 and 1960. These are the flood levels, the highest shown being 15 November 1894; thankfully now a thing of the past after improved flood defences for the city.

ADDRESS Claverton Street, BA2 4LE TIP If you want to avoid the underpass and 'snakes and ladders' staircases at Bath Spa, there is a rear entrance on the Ha'penny Bridge side that goes straight to platform two.

39 Harry Patch Planters

Remembering the last fighting Tommy

Harry Patch lived an extraordinary life. Born in Combe Down in 1898, he fought in World War I at the third battle of Ypres, also known as Passchendaele, in 1917. He and his Lewis gun team were hit by a German shell, with the explosion killing three of his friends and seriously wounding Harry. 'All I can remember was a flash,' he wrote in his autobiography. 'I went down, blew me down I suppose. I saw the blood; I had a field dressing on. I must have passed out. How long I lay there I don't know.' After the war, he worked as a plumber and was a firefighter in Bath during World War II because he was just one year over the conscription age.

It was only towards the end of his life when his story became more widely known. Because by virtue of his longevity – something he put down to not smoking, drinking or gambling – he became the last living man to have fought in the trenches. Known as 'the last fighting Tommy', he began talking more about his experiences when he turned 100. Harry was the oldest man in Europe when he died in 2009 at the age of 111 years, one month, one week and one day.

Two lead planters on either side of Bath's War Memorial were placed there in 2010, having been paid for by members of the public as well as organisations including local businesses and the Bath platoon of the Somerset Army Cadets.

In 2005, Harry was interviewed on BBC Radio 4 with Radiohead frontman Thom Yorke moved to write a song in tribute, 'Harry Patch (In Memory Of)', inspired by the supercentenarian's own words. The song was only the second single by Radiohead to not feature on one of their albums, with all proceeds donated to the Royal British Legion. Former poet laureate Andrew Motion's poem, 'The Death of Harry Patch', marked the veteran's passing, with Motion's words set to music by composer Peter Maxwell Davies in 'The Five Acts of Harry Patch'.

ADDRESS Planters are next to the War Memorial, Royal Avenue, BA1 2PH
TIP A painting of Harry Patch by Bill Leyshon, commissioned by the *Western Daily Press*, is on display at the Bishop's Palace in Wells (www.bishopspalace.org.uk).

40 The Haruspex Stone

Blood, guts, gore and predictions

At the Roman Baths, there is a stone the meaning of which many Romans would have struggled to understand. A haruspex was a priest who predicted the future by examining animal entrails. This was an unusual role and the haruspex in Bath is the only one to have ever been recorded in Roman Britain, showing the significance of Aquae Sulis almost 2,000 years ago.

The haruspex stone was found during an excavation of the site in 1965. It is now on display in the temple courtyard close to the sacrificial altar that was the place of work of Bath's own haruspex: Lucius Marcius Memor. Not everyone believed in his predictions but his work would still have been carried out during special occasions. Even for Romans and before them the Etruscans, this was an old practice that had been established in the East prior to Greco-Roman times. Like tea reading today, this special brand of fortune telling might well have told people what they wanted to know.

On the stone in Bath is an inscription in Latin informing visitors to the temple about Memor's unusual job. But his job was so rare that the abbreviation 'HAR' for haruspex on the centre of the dedication stone itself has had 'VSP' added to it in smaller letters. This may spoil the symmetry of the stone but it makes it clearer for a Roman audience what was going on here. Not wanting to cast aspersions on the professionalism of the carver of this stone, but it also appears that Memor's name originally had the 'o' missing, with it added above the second 'm'. This might signify that Memor asked the carver to correct the stone, with it being hastily edited before being put on display.

In translation, the inscription reads: *To the goddess Sulis, Lucius Marcius Memor, a haruspex, gave as a gift.* Memor's gift to the goddess Sulis Minerva was probably a statue which stood next to the stone, hopefully carved with more care than this unique object.

ADDRESS The Roman Baths, Abbey Church Yard, BA1 1LZ, +44 (0)1225 477785, www.romanbaths.co.uk TIP Also on display in The Roman Baths are curse tablets with messages inscribed on sheets of lead or pewter, which were rolled up and thrown into the spring where the spirit of the goddess Sulis Minerva dwelt.

41 Hedgemead Park

Victorian pleasure grounds from natural disasters

A battlemented lookout tower that could have once been part of an imposing fortress casts a shadow over one section of Hedgemead Park. But the tower wasn't protecting this land from invaders; it is protection from the land itself. This area of Bath is still known as its artisan quarter but there were once many more living in Edgemead on the hill now known as Hedgemead Park. But it was prone to landslips, with a serious incident in 1881 resulting in the council pulling down the most seriously damaged homes. After another major slip occurred in 1883, it was decided that houses must never be built here and the idea for a public park was raised. The first phase of the new Hedgemead Pleasure Grounds opened in 1889, with the Walcot Military Band playing in the new bandstand. The battlemented lookout tower dates back to this time; designed by Thomas Silcock to prevent further landslips.

On what is now the children's play area were once the greenhouses of Bath's parks department. The pride of the original park keeper Theophilus Riddle (who later became the superintendent of all Bath's pleasure grounds and parks), the award-winning plants and flowers grown here graced public buildings across the city. After being badly damaged in the Blitz of 1942, the greenhouses were removed after the war and swings put in their place.

The vertiginous aspect of Hedgemead Park lent itself to an ambitious scheme soon after its creation to build a funicular railway. Plans for a 'Bath Gradient Tramway' were put forward in 1894 by George Croydon Marks, who later became an MP, a knight and a baron. When he was but a humble engineer, albeit a cliff railways specialist, Marks proposed a funicular that would start on London Street and climb up to the back of Camden Crescent Gardens on a level with St Stephen's Road. The council was happy to allow its passage across the park but the scheme was abandoned after the rest of the land was unable to be purchased.

ADDRESS Hedgemead Park, Lansdown Road, BA1 5NG, www.bathnes.gov.uk/visit-hedgemead-park TIP A memorial and tombstone to the Reverend George Austen, the father of Jane, can be found in the graveyard of St Swithin's (www.stswithinswalcot.org.uk) opposite Hedgemead Park.

42 Herschel Astronomy Museum

Uranus was discovered from a house in Bath

William Herschel came to Bath as a musician but left the city as the King's Astronomer. William's sister, Caroline, joined him in Bath from their home in Germany, originally being employed as his assistant but later becoming a renowned astronomer in her own right. What is now the Herschel Museum of Astronomy is where the pair lived and worked. It was in the back garden on the night of 13 March 1781 that William discovered the planet Uranus from his hand-built telescope, doubling the size of the known solar system. He had looked further into space than any other human and Uranus was the first planet to be identified since the days of the Ancient Greeks.

William was the organist of the Octagon Chapel on Milsom Street, the city's director of public concerts and director of the Bath Orchestra, with Caroline often singing solos. Away from music, the brother and sister duo devoted themselves to the study of the stars, building bigger and better telescopes in the house on New King Street that they turned into a workshop. Look out for a mould made of horse dung into which molten metal would have been poured to make telescopic mirrors.

Caroline was also a pioneer. As well as helping William, she was the first woman in the world to discover a comet and the first in Britain to earn a living from astronomy. Thanks to a £50 salary from King George III, she became Britain's first professional female scientist.

William died in 1822 at Observatory House in Slough near Windsor, in whose garden he built what was then the biggest telescope in the world at 40 feet (12 metres) in length, through which his other discoveries included the rotation of Saturn's rings and the existence of infrared radiation. After William's death, Caroline returned to Hanover where she died in 1848 at the age of 97, having continued to catalogue nebulae and star clusters.

ADDRESS 19 New King Street, BA1 2BL, +44 (0)1225 446865, www.herschelmuseum.org.uk TIP Bath Astronomers hold regular stargazing events at Monkton Combe and Alice Park, and loan telescopes to their members (www.bathastronomers.org.uk).

43 J. Ellett Smith & Plumber

An unusual ghost sign

It doesn't take long on a promenade around Bath to be transported back in time thanks to more than a few faded memories from the past. Handpainted advertisements proliferate across the city, allowing you to see what businesses occupied premises long before the current custodians. What are today restaurants, hairdressers and vape shops were previously milliners, reading rooms and brush manufacturers. Bath is not alone in having these 'ghost signs', but it is probably the UK city with the greatest abundance. This is down to a variety of reasons, including the smooth surface of Bath stone, making it ideal for signwriting, and hanging signs creating a hazard for sedan chairs. Hanging signs were banned in Paris in 1761 and other cities soon followed the French capital's lead.

Some ghost signs in Bath are faded almost beyond recognition and even experts do not know what some of the bleached-out letters used to spell. But others are still in glorious technicolour and seem as if they could have been painted yesterday. Look out for the Walcot Fruit & Potato Stores at 6 Walcot Buildings, 'the Asylum for Teaching Young Females Household Work' on Gay's Hill, Brown's haberdashers above Society Café in the Corridor and many, many more.

One ghost sign, however, is very different from the rest. 'J. Ellett, Smith & Plumber' is made not out of paint but of ironwork, positioned above the roof of the business. John Ellett began life as a farmer in Dorset before switching trades to become a blacksmith by the 1851 census, helped by his eldest sons Thomas and Henry. The family relocated to Bath but by 1881 it was John's widow Ann who was carrying on the business as A. Ellett & Sons. The surviving sign was commissioned by one of John and Ann's other sons, also called John, to serve the dual purpose of both advertising his company and demonstrating his blacksmithing skills.

ADDRESS 11 Beauford Square, BA1 1HJ **TIP** Bath's first plaque dedicated to a ghost sign can be found at 15 Abbey Church Yard, the former premises of Rodway's Wholesale & Retail Straw & Millinery Rooms.

44 Jewish Burial Ground

A fascinating cross-section of Bath life

Hidden away behind high stone walls in Combe Down is the only remaining physical site of Bath's once-thriving 19th-century Jewish community. The first burial on land that had previously been a surface quarry took place here in 1812 for Sarah Moses. No burial register has survived but researchers have identified around 80 men, women and children who are buried here. They include Kate Aaron (1827–1901) who was born in Dover and worked with her three sisters as an assistant to their father, clothier Jacob Reuben. Kate married jeweller Samuel Aaron from Torquay and they set up shop at 6 Broad Street. Also buried here is Levy Zachariah, who died at 96 Hanover Street aged 93 in 1861. Before moving to Bath, he was an importer and dealer in fancy goods in London. It is only presumed that Levy is buried here alongside his niece, Elizabeth, because the tombstone next to hers has lost its inscription.

The youngest person known to be buried here according to the headstones is Minnie Tyler, who was just two years old when she died in 1898. Minnie's mother Freda and father Simon were both born in Russia. Of their six children, only two lived beyond childhood.

In recent years, the Friends of Bath Jewish Burial Ground have been working to protect its history, atmosphere and physical character. 'In practical terms this means maximum retention of the historic fabric with minimal intervention, involving repair and restoration where necessary rather than replacement,' they explain on their website. 'The approach is not to change the site but to restore where necessary so that the heritage is preserved for future generations.'

Close to the entrance gates is a single-storey building that predates the burial ground. Once a small cottage, it was home to poor families – some of whom were also the cemetery's caretakers until the last resident moved out in 1929.

ADDRESS 1 Greendown Place, Combe Down, BA2 5DD, www.bathjewishburialground.org TIP As its name suggests, Entry Hill in Combe Down was originally the ancient Roman gateway into Bath. It is now a park after previously being a landfill site and a golf course.

45 K6 Telephone Kiosk

A rare muted example of a usually red ringer

The red telephone box is as much a British symbol as fish and chips and Wallace and Gromit. So to find a mostly battleship grey version of the familiar structure is rather discombobulating. This particular version is a K6 telephone kiosk designed by Sir Giles Gilbert Scott in 1935 to mark King George V's jubilee. It was one of around 60,000 to be installed across the UK and in some overseas territories by the General Post Office (GPO) between 1936 and 1968, but only a very few were painted in grey.

The reason for the reduction of red on this one is that despite being seen as intrinsically English today, there was originally much discontent over their 'intrusive' bright features, in particular from members of the Royal Fine Art Commission – a design watchdog founded at the behest of Queen Victoria's husband Prince Albert that advised on the quality of public projects. So in areas of either natural or architectural beauty such as this Bath vista overlooking the Royal Crescent, the GPO bowed to pressure and allowed kiosks to be painted in either grey or green, with the glazing bars over the windows on this K6 in Bath 'picked out' in red. It's 8 feet (2.5 metres) high and three feet wide; you can tell you are looking at a K6 thanks to a number of unique design features, including a moulded royal crown in the pediment above a once-illuminated telephone sign.

If you fancy finding a few other rare surviving examples of grey K6 kiosks, the one in Kilmersdon in Somerset is now used as a book swap, and there is another similar example in the village of Blaenwaun in Carmarthenshire that contains a defibrillator. And if you're really keen, on display at the National Telephone Kiosk Collection at Avoncroft Museum in Worcestershire is every type of telephone kiosk used from 1912 to the present day, including the navy-blue police call box now better known as Doctor Who's Tardis.

ADDRESS Brock Street, BA1 2LW (what3words: leaned.speech.seated)
TIP Look inside the kiosk for a reproduction of a 1769 painting by Thomas Malton from almost exactly this spot, showing the Royal Crescent under construction.

46 King Bladud and his Pigs

Wallowing in warm mud

Rome has Romulus and Remus as the city's legendary founders. Bath has King Bladud and his pigs. You may think that the Romans founded the place they called Aquae Sulis but other accounts credit Bladud with its discovery and foundation in 836 BC, ably assisted by his happy herd of mud-loving livestock.

The story goes that when he was a young prince, Bladud travelled to Athens, where he contracted leprosy. On his return to England, he was shunned by society and became a swineherd (somebody who looks after pigs – rather than a shepherd who looks after sheep). His new job is remembered in the village of Swainswick, where he is said to have stayed; and Swineford, where he crossed the River Avon. It was his pigs wallowing in warm mud that brought a change in Bladud's fortunes. For his animals also suffered from leprosy, which was miraculously cured following their sloshing about in the mire. Giving it a go too, Bladud was also healed. He returned to his family with news of the healing waters, founded the town of Bath on the spot and was crowned the ninth king of the Britons.

A statue of King Bladud in Parade Gardens carved in 1859 by Stefano Valerio Pieroni was joined by a pig in 2009 sculpted by Nigel Bryant, stone conservation lecturer at City of Bath College, and a group of his students. Their happy porker was a version in Bath stone of more than 100 others that had gone on display across Bath the previous summer as part of a citywide sculpture trail (www.kingbladudspigs.org).

Also within Parade Gardens, look out for the remains of Monks Mill, a medieval mill that is older than Bath Abbey. Built in the 13th century, Monks Mill was one of two mills outside the city walls on opposite sides of the River Avon. The historic ruin is believed to be one of only two of Bath's remaining early medieval structures, the other being the abbey's Norman foundations.

ADDRESS Parade Gardens, Grand Parade, BA2 4DF, www.bathnes.gov.uk/visit-parade-gardens TIP The Bladud's Head pub in Larkhall is just one of several places in the city named after the legendary king.

47 Ladymead Fountain

Early example of a free public drinking fountain

We take it for granted today that clean and safe running water is always available with just a twist of a tap. But it was not always like this. Even in Bath that was founded because of water, clean liquid to drink was still not commonplace until the 1900s. While wealthy Georgians might have employed professional water carriers known as 'cobs' to bring clean water to their homes, most of the population had to go themselves to wells or rivers in order to collect water to drink or with which to wash.

It was only in the Victorian era that water fountains became prevalent, with many constructed during this period still on our streets; although few still fulfil their original function. The very first drinking fountain still stands next to St Sepulchre-without-Newgate church in the Holborn district of London, having been erected by the Metropolitan Drinking Fountain and Cattle Trough Association in 1859. Their stated aim was to be 'the only agency for providing free supplies of water for man and beast in the streets of London'. Their vital work could not just be restricted to the capital, however, and only one year later, the Ladymead Fountain was built in Bath to a design by city architect Charles Edward Davis that lent heavily on the one at St Sepulchre.

The Ladymead Fountain is not subtle. Set into the steep retaining wall of the Bladud Buildings' back gardens, it was constructed close to the site of an earlier conduit and was originally both a trough and drinking fountain consisting of a variety of different stones, including grey and pink sandstone, white marble, and polished pink and grey granite. According to Art UK, the Ladymead Fountain's medley of stones is 'indicative of the High Victorian taste for architectural polychromy and interest in geology'; with Davis also influenced by John Ruskin's depictions of Venetian medieval architecture.

ADDRESS Walcot Street, BA1 5BD (what3words: basic.transit.verbs) TIP Landrace on Walcot Street next to Ladymead Fountain is a Michelin Guide-recommended artisan bakery, café, pizzeria and restaurant (www.landrace.co.uk).

48 Lansdown Crescent

And its resident flock of sheep

Think of Bath's grandest boulevard and what springs to mind? Probably the Royal Crescent. It certainly ticks all of the boxes: a monumental half-ellipse, strict uniformity, famous former residents.

But head up the hill a bit from the Royal Crescent and you will find Lansdown Crescent. Smaller, yes, but forming almost one-third of a circle with strict uniformity and famous former residents. Its more illustrious neighbour may have hosted a concert by Robbie Williams on its front lawn in 2025 but what it doesn't have is its own flock of resident sheep. The sheep on the steep slope in front of Lansdown Crescent have, for the last three decades, belonged to farmer Douglas Creed from the village of Kelston, just a few miles north-west of Bath. The Suffolk mule-cross lambs are born in mid-April and then moved from the farm to Lansdown Crescent, where they are sometimes small enough to squeeze through the railings onto the road, until they return to the bleating of their concerned mothers. Both the ewes and their lambs remain in the field as long as the grass is at a suitable length for them. In the lower part of the field, a white plastic tub contains a cereal-based compound enriched with molasses and minerals to supplement the animals' grassy diet. When the grass has all been eaten, the sheep have to be moved elsewhere until the circle of life starts again the following year.

Lansdown Crescent was designed by John Palmer for coach-builder and developer Charles Spackman, and built between 1789 and 1793. William Beckford lived here, from where he rode daily to his tower. *Pevsner's Architectural Guide to Bath* calls the road's convex-concave-convex plan 'remarkable' and its presence 'unrivalled'. 'Historically, the crescent in winter would have floated, seemingly on clouds, above a pall of blue smoke from thousands of lodging-house chimneys.'

ADDRESS Lansdown Crescent, BA1 5EX **TIP** Royal Crescent is not actually 100 per cent uniform. The front door at number 22 has been painted yellow since 1972, when resident Amabel Wellesley-Colley successfully defended herself in a public enquiry to keep the colour.

49 Little Theatre Cinema

A cinephile's paradise

On the top floor of the Little Theatre Cinema are photographs of happy couples who have chosen to get married here. There's Matt and Keshia standing in front of the main doors, Lorna and Lewis sitting in the box office, and Peter and Julie covered in confetti thrown in the main auditorium. The fact that people choose to have their nuptials here shows the special place this two-screen cinema has had in the hearts of Bath's cinephiles for almost a century. Grab a snack, a beer or glass of wine from the bar downstairs, settle back in your seat and enjoy the films, with baby- and dog-friendly screenings among the regular programming.

The Cinema Treasures website calls the Little Theatre Cinema a 'cosy little gem... lovely and very old fashioned'. It's tucked away in a small square and has been immortalised in celluloid for all time thanks to its appearance in *Fantastic Mr Fox*. Director Wes Anderson is said to have scouted the location ahead of the release of the 2009 film based on the book by Roald Dahl. Cinemagoers in the Little Theatre cheered when watching the film on the big screen and seeing the venue in which they were sitting.

When this cinema opened in 1935, it was a news theatre with temporary Bath resident, Ethiopian emperor Haile Selassie, a regular visitor. Selassie and his entourage would watch newsreels of the Italian invasion of their homeland from the balcony in the main auditorium, which became known as the royal box. Feature films were first shown in 1939, the first two being *Peg of Old Drury* and *Oh, Mr Porter*. In 1979, the former scenery store and lounge area were converted into a second screen. While other cinemas around it have closed (The Egg theatre, for example, was formerly the Robins, and The Forum also originally opened as a cinema), the Little Theatre Cinema has continued by hook, by crook and with lots of love.

ADDRESS St Michael's Place, BA1 1SG, +44 (0)871 902 5735, www.picturehouses.com/cinema/little-theatre-cinema **TIP** In 2026, the Everyman on Dorchester Street was named by *Time Out* as the 57th best in their list of the 100 greatest cinemas in the world (www.everymancinema.com).

50 London Plane Trees

Standing strong in some auspicious locations

The London plane tree that stands proudly on Abbey Green was planted in 1880 to mark the marriage of Sarah Jefferys, who lived at number 2 with her chimney sweep dad Thomas. Contrary to rumours, it was never used for hangings of either convicted criminals or women who were thought to be witches. 'Its great size could have been hastened by its roots reaching into the spring feeding the nearby Roman baths,' writes Paul Wood, the author of *Tree Hunting: 1,000 Trees to Find in Britain and Ireland's Towns and Cities.* But this author was not able to verify the validity of that particular fact, or whether Bath's London planes are actually among the world's oldest architecturally planted trees, which has also been widely claimed.

It is remarkable to think that when The Circus was built, the grand trees that now stand in its centre had yet to be planted and were not even planned, but are now considerably larger than the buildings that surround them. The circular centre of The Circus was originally paved with stone setts above a covered reservoir. Architect John Wood the Elder even envisaged 'the exhibition of sports' here but instead these three London plane trees that were seedlings in 1800 now form a central showpiece that from above looks as if a small forest has been planted in this most auspicious of locations.

Look out for more majestic London planes in Alice Park, Newton Road and the aptly named London Road. The best way to discover many of Bath's most significant trees is via Bath Urban Treescape (www.bathurbantreescape.com) in either paper or digital form. A number of walking trails are available, focusing on different areas of the city, from 'Treemendous Twerton' to 'Combe Down Canopy'. The first Bath Urban Treescape identification plaque was unveiled in 2024 on the London plane tree in Abbey Green – the only tree to feature on more than one of the trails.

ADDRESS Abbey Green, BA1 1NW & The Circus, BA1 2EW TIP The Crystal Palace pub on Abbey Green is run by Fuller's Brewery in a building that dates from 1654 (www.crystalpalacepub.co.uk).

51 Magalleria

Showcasing the vitality of independent magazines

There is something incredibly satisfying about a shop selling just magazines at a time when even your glasses or watch can distract you with notifications. Among all the advances in digital technology, magazines continue to thrive. There is less gatekeeping with magazines than in book publishing; if you want to create a beautiful magazine about your niche interests, then nothing is stopping you.

Magalleria feels more like a bookshop than a newsagent. It also stocks all of the available back issues of the magazines on their shelves, in case you find a new favourite and want to catch up. What that new favourite will be could be one of thousands to catch your eye in a shop overflowing with lovingly curated printed material from publishers across the world. Magalleria has already outgrown one shop to move into bigger premises, having first opened in 2015 on Broad Street before moving to Upper Borough Walls in 2021. They pride themselves on stocking 'arguably the widest range of independently published, premium, rare and specialised magazines you'll find anywhere'.

Inside, a large central table features an always-eclectic variety of titles. On a recent visit, among the delights on this table were *Mushroom People*, a special edition, single-issue magazine for mycophiles; *What Women Create*, with this edition having a particular focus on ceramic art; and *Catnip*, 'a magazine for cat people'.

In *The Handbook of Magazine Studies*, Megan Le Masurier writes in her chapter 'Slow Magazines' that in a shop like Magalleria, 'small scale, beautifully designed print magazines subvert, critique and sometimes utterly confound… mainstream categories by using the magazine format to provide alternative representations of the way we live, think and create'. Digital and print can co-exist. But the best place to read a magazine is in the printed form, not on your phone.

ADDRESS 5 Upper Borough Walls, BA1 1RG, +44 (0)7810 778758, store.magalleria.co.uk **TIP** Above Magalleria is Asian fusion restaurant Bonghy Bo, which has been serving food from Japan, China and Thailand since 1987 (www.bonghybo.com).

52 Mary Shelley's House of Frankenstein

A multi-sensory museum

You might think you know Frankenstein, but how well do you *really* know Frankenstein? And what is the link to Bath? The short answer appears on a sign outside the Pump Room stating that the novel *Frankenstein* by Mary Shelley was written right here between 1816 and 1817. Mary Wollstonecraft Godwin had arrived in Bath aged 19 in September 1816 and took lodgings at 5 Abbey Churchyard – later demolished to make way for the Pump Room extension in the 1890s. In the nearby Kingston Lecture Room, young Mary attended scientific lectures by Dr Wilkinson, whose suggestion that one day electricity might be used to bring inanimate matter to life resonated with Mary, who had recently been experiencing nightmares during thunderstorms.

After marrying poet Percy Shelley in December 1816, Mary left Bath in early 1817, by which time she had written much of the novel that was published anonymously in London in January 1818. Coincidentally, under the sign on Abbey Churchyard there is now an electricity sub-station that delivers thousands of volts to central Bath.

To learn more about the mysterious Mary Shelley and her world-famous creation, a multi-sensory museum tells the story of *Frankenstein*'s inspiration. There are jump-scares along the way, artefacts aplenty and even two Frankenstein-themed escape rooms. Plus an eight-foot animatronic model of the monster that the museum claims is a world-first for being authentically reproduced exactly as Shelley described. The model of Victor Frankenstein's creature was made in collaboration with Chris Goodman from BAFTA award-winning special effects company Millennium FX. Be prepared to come face to face with a living and breathing Frankenstein that once again has come to life after its unusual origins in 19th-century Bath.

ADDRESS 37 Gay Street, BA1 2NT, +44 (0)1225 551542, www.houseoffrankenstein.com
TIP The Jane Austen Centre and Thirsty Meeples board game café are both near neighbours on Gay Street.

53 Medieval Walls

A few fortifications still remain

Best known for his diary that gives an account of the Great Fire of London in 1666, Samuel Pepys visited Bath two years after that, when he reported that the city's wall was in good condition. In the following decades, however, it gradually fell into decay until it was almost completely demolished in the 18th century as it was a hindrance to expansion. The best-preserved section of the wall above ground is at rampart level on Upper Borough Walls (the city wall was also known as the borough walls), which was accurately restored in the late 19th century. The surviving wall marking the northern boundary of the medieval city looks almost too good to be true, with seven crenellations on top for added authenticity. Head down Trim Street to get a view of the wall from the other side. It is higher here – the wall was once more than 20 feet (6 metres) tall and 10 feet (3 metres) wide – with a plaque indicating this small section survived because the burial ground for Bath General Hospital lay just outside it.

Once again (perhaps unfairly) comparing Bath to London, the capital's Roman-built wall surrounded 134 hectares of land whereas the area inside Bath's walls was just 10 hectares. After remaining essential to the defence of the city up until the English Civil War in 1651, those forward-thinking Georgians did not manage to get rid of all of the wall; it's just that much of it is now underground and contained within a number of basements. One section of existing wall is buried beneath Terrace Walk, while 1 North Parade has a wall built off the medieval wall's foundations.

Above ground, it's possible to find another visible section of city wall hidden next to the former Marks & Spencer delivery area along North Parade Buildings, with the lower section of masonry believed to be part of the original Roman structure that has been here since the 4th century.

ADDRESS Upper Borough Walls, BA1 4HB TIP Follow the route of the wall in *An Historical Map of Bath*, published by the Historic Towns Trust, which covers the medieval, Stuart and Georgian city (www.historictownstrust.uk/maps/an-historical-map-of-bath).

54 'The Min'

Former hospital waiting to be transformed

Head down Parsonage Lane and you will walk underneath a two-storey bridge that once connected a Georgian 'country house' hospital with its extension built over a century later. You will also see the stained-glass windows in the hospital's chapel. And you will see shoots of greenery surrounding the building, which is an indication that not much has happened here for a good few years.

Singapore-based property developer Fragrance Group bought the former hospital for £21.5 million in 2018 and in 2021 they were granted planning permission to convert the building into a 167-bed luxury hotel. Progress has been painfully slow so far, however, and paying guests are unlikely to be staying where patients once took Bath's famous waters for several years yet.

Opened in 1742 on the site of a former theatre as the General Hospital, it then became the Royal Mineral Water Hospital – where its nickname as 'The Min' comes from – before later becoming the Royal National Hospital for Rheumatic Diseases. In the 20th century, this was one of the leading hospitals in the world for the treatment of arthritic and rheumatic ailments, with the medical expertise moving the short distance to the Royal United Hospital in Weston when this city centre site closed in 2019.

The great and the good of Georgian Bath were behind the foundation of the hospital designed by John Wood the Elder. Ralph Allen donated all the stone from his quarry at Combe Down, and his close friend Beau Nash, Bath's master of ceremonies, wasted no opportunity to tap up wealthy visitors and locals alike. But the hospital was not for residents, nor those who had travelled to the city. Instead, the renowned spa waters were used as treatments for the 'well recommended' poor and needy from across the country, with accommodation and care for as long as was needed, paid for by the hospital's wealthy benefactors.

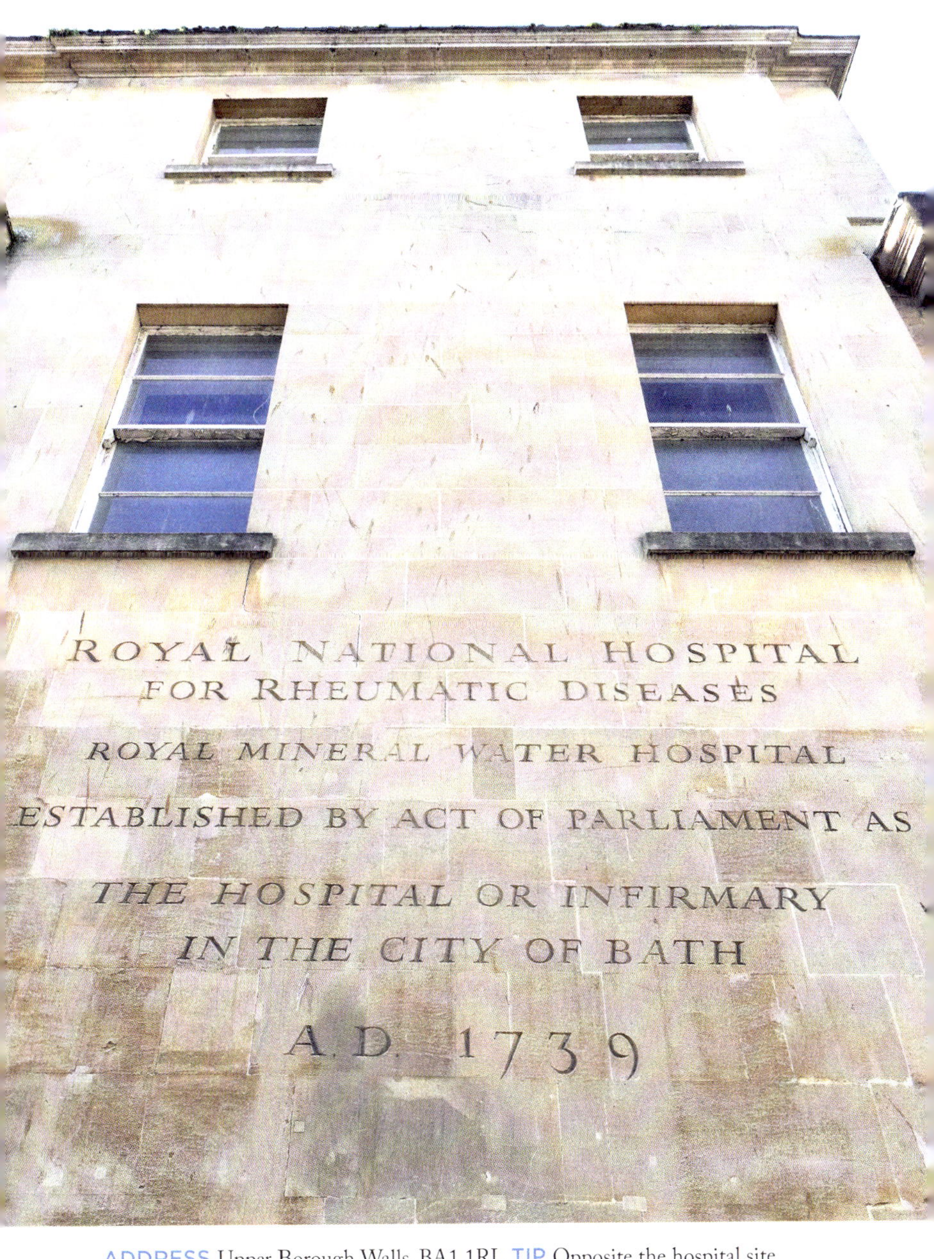

ADDRESS Upper Borough Walls, BA1 1RL TIP Opposite the hospital site is Trim Bridge, formed in 1728 as a public passage for carriages to Queen Square.

55 Monkton Combe Lock-Up

Temporary imprisonment for local miscreants

Once upon a time, if you found yourself in trouble in Monkton Combe you would probably have been thrown into the lock-up. There are two cells inside, one of which has only a few small holes to let air in during the time of imprisonment, lasting from overnight to up to a couple of days. In both Somerset and Wiltshire, the village lock-up was known as a 'blind house' because they were windowless. There was no particularly kind treatment for those inside; men, women and children could all have been apprehended on suspicion of having committed a crime, or for being drunk and disorderly.

This lock-up dating from around 1776 has a domed roof and a door with a peep hole for checking on its temporary residents. One theory as to why it is located away from the centre of the village is that it was placed close to the Somerset Coal Canal. While the canal was being built, its navvies may have become the lock-up's regular inmates after spending their wages in the local pub and subsequently getting into trouble.

According to Prison History, a project created by historians at the Open University, lock-ups were 'a gateway to the criminal justice system as well as an expression of justice at the local level. They were important local institutions'. People imprisoned in a lock-up would either have been taken to a magistrate who decided if they were to face trial, pay a fine or go to prison; or they would have been released back into the community, 'their short confinement, according to local opinion, having served as punishment enough'.

Another lock-up can be found on Bath Road in the village of Kelston. Less is known about this one but it is also believed to date from the late 18th century. Constructed of coursed squared rubble, it has a plank door with an iron grille, locks and hinges. Inside, there are two vaulted compartments – but you would not want to stay here for long.

ADDRESS 1 Station Cottage, Mill Lane, Monkton Combe, BA2 7HD TIP The Wheelwrights Arms pub and guesthouse in Monkton Combe is named after the craftsmen who once built and repaired cart wheels nearby (www.wheelwrightsarmsbath.com).

56 Mumu

A freed African slave who was born a princess

A grave in Locksbrook Cemetery bears the inscription: *In Memory of Mumu, a deaf and dumb African girl. She was rescued in childhood from a slave vessel and taken to the Church Missionary School at Charlotte, Sierra Leone, from whence she was sent to England for education and remained 11 years in the Bath Institute for the Blind and Deaf and Dumb. She was baptised Dec 29th 1857 and received the Christian names of Annie Jane Elwin. After a short illness, she fell asleep in Jesus, May 16th 1866, aged 25 years.*

Mumu is not the only name on this headstone that also remembers other former residents at the institution, founded in 1843 and located at 8–9 Walcot Parade; with the Deaf & Dumb Industrial Home at 13 Walcot Parade. (It must be remembered that the original meaning of 'dumb' meant silent or unable to speak, and the term was used in a non-offensive way, unlike its present-day connotations.) Marked on Mumu's headstone is also George Spear, 'a blind boy, a native of Cape Palmas, W. Africa' who died in 1866 at the age of 11; Anne Toone, who died in 1866 aged 13; Eliza Feldwick, who died in 1872 aged 13; and Mary Emma Pearce, who died in 1872 with no age given on the grave but who was also 13 according to research by Philip Bendall.

Mumu – whose real name has been lost – was born a princess but kidnapped by slavers after her father was murdered. In the *Quarterly Review of Deaf Mute Education* from October 1892, Mumu was said to have 'very soon made rapid progress in her lessons' after arriving in Bath. She was described as being 'of a very amiable, teachable and affectionate disposition'. After finishing her schooling, she worked in London but later returned to Bath, where sadly she died after a short illness far from her original home. According to the article from 1892, 'she died beloved and regretted by her friends, teachers and companions'.

ADDRESS Locksbrook Cemetery, Cedric Road, Lower Weston, BA1 3PD
TIP Locksbrook Cemetery contains 90 World War I graves, 44 of which form a plot next to a large cross.

57 Newton St Loe Castle

A seat of learning in royal grounds

Bath Spa University prides itself on its modern facilities. But some undergraduates still find themselves studying within a 14th-century tower on its main campus in Newton Park to the west of the city. The fortified tower is often referred to as the central keep of a former castle. It makes sense, being part of a building known as Newton St Loe Castle. But this is actually a surviving section not of a castle but of a fortified manor house dating originally from the 1300s, which has been much altered and remodelled over the subsequent centuries. It remains a striking addition to the landscape, however, and a unique part of the university's campus.

Coats of arms and gargoyles look down from the three-storey tower, which also has a vaulted basement where one rumour says King John was kept prisoner. Look closely and a V-mark indicates the existence of a former wing. Inside, the room on the third floor has a 17th-century freestone fireplace that you might be lucky to glimpse through an open door. Members of the public can walk inside the tower and up the staircase but the rooms remain private.

Newton Park was designed by landscape architect Lancelot 'Capability' Brown in the 18th century to complement a new mansion being built on the grounds. The park today features a nature reserve, lake, woods and rolling fields, alongside the tower and other listed buildings including a gatehouse, stables and dairy.

Bath Spa University can trace its own history back to the establishment of Bath School of Art in 1852. Howard Hodgkin was one of the students when it changed its name to the Bath Academy of Art. Bath Spa's Newton Park campus began as Newton Park Teacher Training College in 1946, training women to become teachers due to a post-war shortage. Today, the university leases the land from the Duchy of Cornwall, which owns the park and nearby village of Newton St Loe.

ADDRESS Bath Spa University, Newton Park, Newton St Loe, BA2 9BN
TIP Newton Farm in Newton St Loe is a traditional mixed farm with a farm shop on site (www.newtonfarmfoods.co.uk).

58 Odd Down Cycle Circuit

Clip on your helmet and off you go

If you are heading on two wheels to Odd Down, prepare to go up. It will serve as a good warm-up for your laps of the Odd Down Cycle Circuit, a mile long (1.5 kilometre) course that skirts some of the pitches at Odd Down Sports Ground. For a couple of pounds you can book a one-hour session at the track. Just remember to bring your helmet as you try your best to recreate Tom Pidcock's cornering techniques in the Tour de France around two tight bends and a pair of 180-degree turns that make up the course.

Helmet on and entry fee paid in the café, make your way to the track via a wooden gate, climb on your trusty steed and away you go. Close to the start, there is a house on Bloomfield Road with a tower built onto the side of it – thought to have enabled a quarry owner to supervise the operations in his adjacent quarry. Now, however, it acts as a handy wayfinder during the laps as it remains somewhere to aim from the furthest corner of the course. Imagine your name written on the track in chalk and the sound of cowbells following you round during your session. This is a rare opportunity for pure cycling with no petrol-guzzling cars or pesky pedestrians to worry about.

The track opened in 2013 thanks to a £600,000 grant from British Cycling. When Olympic gold medallist Dani King officially opened the facility, it was one of only 17 specific closed-road cycling circuits in England. Every Saturday morning, the Sulis Scorpions (www.sulisscorpions.co.uk) host coaching and training sessions on the track for cyclists aged 7 to 18. If road cycling is a little too sedate for you, then also at Odd Down is the Tumps BMX track, home to Bath BMX Club (www.bathbmxclub.com). Members and non-members can use the BMX track and there are also regular coaching sessions, with club riders regularly using their skills first learned in Bath at national, European and world championships.

ADDRESS Odd Down Sports Centre, Chelwood Drive, Odd Down, BA2 2PR, +44 (0)1225 300420, www.better.org.uk/leisure-centre/banes/odd-down-sports-ground/cycling **TIP** Running races also take place around the Odd Down circuit, including the annual BTC 5k with a field of elite runners and others just going for PBs (www.bristoltrackclub.com/our-events).

59 Old King Edward's School

'It looks like it has been used as an ashtray'

There is an entrance to Shires Yard next to the former King Edward's School. A cast-iron gate takes you to one of the city's most exclusive environs, promising 'a perfect hidden oasis in which to unwind, away from Bath's bustling crowds'. But before you enjoy the seasonal produce in Root, have a suit fitted in Gieves & Hawkes or get your boots polished in R. M. Williams, pause a minute to look more closely at what you have just walked by.

Among Bath's buildings of international prestige, this one has long been an embarrassment. While neighbouring Shires Yard is glittering opulence, the long-derelict site that was once King Edward's School has previously been described as looking 'like it has been used as an ashtray'. It is the only building in Bath on Historic England's Heritage at Risk Register, meaning that it has been assessed as 'most at risk of being lost as a result of neglect, decay or inappropriate development'.

The issue with the listed building on Broad Street is that it has simply been left to decline by its owners, Yorkshire-based brewery Samuel Smith – who promised to convert it into a hotel, but have done nothing. Vacant since the 1980s, the Bath Preservation Trust has made attempts to ensure that something happens here. But so far their efforts have been fruitless.

It was former deputy council leader Richard Samuel who said in 2023: 'The owners of this building are not looking after it and it is on the national risk register and that is a disgrace for a city like this.' Samuel said he walked past the former school every day and had watched its decline.

The council pledged to 'assist in expediting the delivery of a suitable scheme' for the building that was the home of King Edward's School from 1754 to 1959, with the school's current site on North Road in Bathwick thriving, unlike their sadly neglected former premises.

ADDRESS 10 Broad Street, BA1 5LJ TIP Directly opposite the former King Edward's School is Broad Street Townhouse: a pub, restaurant and boutique hotel (www.butcombe.com/broad-street-townhouse-bath).

60 Old Theatre Royal

The most important theatre outside London

Although its usage has changed over the centuries, a visitor to the Old Theatre Royal today can still see traces of when the building was a theatre, particularly as the original stage and backstage areas remain intact. It was not just any theatre either. This was once the most important theatre outside of London when, in 1768, it became the first provincial theatre to be granted a royal patent. In the years before that, what had opened in 1750 as the St James Theatre had operated as Bath's first purpose-built playhouse. A repertory company performed the same plays here and in its sister venue, the Theatre Royal in Bristol. Actors, stagehands and sets travelled between the two cities. One of the most famous actors to have performed in that company was Sarah Siddons, well-known for her portrayal of Lady Macbeth. A plaque outside Bath's former theatre remembers her 'renowned' ability.

Like the plays performed here, the building has had a number of different acts. The £1,000 cost of erecting the theatre had been covered by the sale of 20 £50 shares, which gave their owners a silver ticket for any night they wished to attend, as well as a small share of box office profits. In 1805, a new Theatre Royal was created in Beauford Square and this Theatre Royal was closed. It remained empty until 1809, when it became a Catholic chapel. A level floor was created over the theatre pit, boxes were removed and replaced with pews, and dressing rooms were converted into school rooms. In 1863, the congregation moved into the new St John's Church and in 1865 this building was purchased by Bath Freemasons, who converted it into the Masonic Hall that remains their home today.

Go on a tour of the building to see two of its five floors, including the Masonic Temple and the vaulted cellars where exiled French nobility were once buried, and that now house a Masonic museum.

ADDRESS Masonic Hall, Old Orchard Street, BA1 1JU, +44 (0)1225 462233, www.oldtheatreroyal.com **TIP** The Pearl of India restaurant occupies a first-floor space on Quiet Street that was originally the mid 19th-century Auction Market & Bazaar and was also once a chapel (www.pearlofindia.co.uk).

61 Our Lady and St Alphege

'It cannot fail to astonish and delight'

Sir Giles Gilbert Scott is best known as the architect of Liverpool Cathedral and the designer of the classic red telephone box – a rare grey version of which can be found in Bath. He described Our Lady and St Alphege Church as one of his favourite commissions but it was originally planned to have the addition of a large bell tower, or campanile, that has never been constructed.

The Catholic church was built to serve the growing population to the south of Bath. The nave and chancel were constructed between 1927 and 1929 but the entire church was not consecrated until 1954 – a nice round 1,000 years after the birth of Alphege, who was born and had been a monk in Bath. Alphege later became abbot of Bath's Anglo-Saxon monastery, then bishop of Winchester and was archbishop of Canterbury when he was murdered by the Danes in 1022. Following a fundraising appeal, a new stained-glass window remembering Alphege and his martyrdom is due to be installed in Bath Abbey's St Alphege Chapel in 2026.

Our Lady and St Alphege was modelled on the much larger Santa Maria in the Rome suburb of Cosmedin, which *Pevsner's Architectural Guide to Bath* describes as 'a severe Early Christian basilica of impressive simplicity'. Inspired by a recent visit to Italy, Scott distilled the main elements of that building into a much smaller parish church, with work continuing on the building until 1960. Pevsner author Michael Forsyth calls Our Lady and St Alphege 'one of Bath's least known post-Georgian buildings, tucked away in an uneventful late C19 suburb', adding that 'it cannot fail to astonish and delight'.

Scott's own description is as follows: 'The church was my first essay into the Romanesque style of architecture. It has always been one of my favourite works; my only regret is that it has not proved possible to complete the exterior by building the campanile.'

ADDRESS Oldfield Lane, Oldfield Park, BA2 3NR, +44 (0)1225 424894, www.saintalphege.org.uk **TIP** A statue of Mary called *Our Lady of Bath, Queen of Peace* was carved onsite in the garden of St John the Evangelist Church on South Parade from a single block of Portland stone.

62 The Packhorse

'The product of a thousand generous hands'

Four hundred years after it first served punters in 1618, The Packhorse once again flung open its doors. This time it was a community-owned pub having been bought back from a property developer. The names of its hundreds of co-owners are on display here with a plaque thanking volunteers, professionals and companies who gifted their time because they passionately believed this pub deserved another chapter. It was the culmination of a four-year campaign to bring the pub back to life. 'The Packhorse, as you see it today, truly is the product of a thousand generous hands,' says the plaque. Ahead of the eighth anniversary of the reopening in 2026, an Instagram post said the Packhorse 'is proof of what a community can do when it comes together'.

Within just two years of its new start, however, it needed to shut its doors again because of the pandemic. A photograph shows 18 people standing socially distanced outside the front door, remembering when The Packhorse was converted into a general supplies shop. With things back to normal, there are now talks, a knitting group, curry nights and guided walks.

On a recent Saturday afternoon in one of the ground-floor rooms of The Packhorse, a father scrolled on his phone while sipping a pint as his two boys busied themselves with some colouring, a young couple appeared to be in the early stages of their relationship ('I don't like small talk,' he told her), a man tapped away on his laptop in one corner, while in another a damp visitor who had missed his bus stop and accidentally ended up a mile's walk away along country lanes warmed his jacket by a roaring fire. Above the fire is a rope; a snapped rope in fact. This is the trophy of a biennial tug of war competition between the villages of Midford and South Stoke. Win or lose, competitors can now join each other again for a post-match pint in The Packhorse.

ADDRESS Old School Hill, South Stoke, BA2 7DU, +44 (0)1225 830300, www.packhorsebath.co.uk TIP Bath's oldest pub is the Saracens Head on Broad Street, which was built in 1713 and where Charles Dickens is reputed to have stayed (www.greeneking.co.uk/pubs/somerset/saracens-head).

63 Parish Boundary Markers

Complicated and troublesome geography

Stand in front of 27 The Paragon today and you will see five letters that have been chiselled almost above the front door: W.P.S.P.P. These are actually two distinct acronyms: W.P. for Walcot Parish and S.P.P. for St Peter & St Paul, also known as Bath Abbey. Elsewhere on the side of a building you might come across S.M.P. for St Michael's, another of the city's parishes. These mix of letters are parish boundary markers, delineating the precise borders of parishes. It was once extremely important to know which one you lived in because you would have had to contribute financially to the upkeep of the parish, with your rates going towards such important matters as street cleaning, poor relief and even an early form of policing.

A stroll along Upper Borough Walls from Trim Bridge will elicit numerous discoveries of more parish boundary markers, attesting to the complicated nature of the boundary at the northernmost edge of what was originally the walled city.

Making one's way from one parish boundary marker to another was once an annual tradition for parishioners, known as 'beating the bounds', with this tradition occasionally resurrected in recent years. By all accounts the historic perambulations were jovial and even debauched affairs. In 1817, there was a disaster when a crowd taking part arrived at the Dolemeads, where a boat was to carry them across the river to South Parade. But too many tried to board the vessel, at which point it capsized, throwing 30 people into the water and resulting in the death by drowning of six poor souls.

Stand once again in front of 27 The Paragon and count your lucky stars that you were not one of the three men who, during a perambulation of Walcot in 1863, had to follow the boundary regardless of what was in the way; this necessitated climbing over this house, which has four storeys at the front and six at the rear.

ADDRESS Various locations including 27 The Paragon, BA1 5LY; at the corner of Trim Bridge and Upper Borough Walls, BA1 1RJ; and on one of the gateposts at the top of Ralph Allen Drive (what3words: unable.lights.chained) TIP The first St Swithin's Church on The Paragon was built soon after 971. In medieval times, Walcot was a hamlet outside the walls of Bath but was encompassed within the enlarged city boundary in 1590.

64 Paying on the Nail

The origin of a famous phrase

There's a lot to be said for the phrase 'it is said': neither confirming nor denying a fact; instead introducing a soupçon of ambiguity. So chapeau to the anonymous writer of the words on a wooden plaque on top of a stone pillar within Guildhall Market. The plaque explains: *This eighteenth century pillar or "nail" stood on the site of the present markets in 1768 for the transaction of business and for prompt payment in bargaining. It is said that this gave origin to the phrase "pay on the nail".*

That phrase 'it is said' does some heavy lifting here as there are at least two other locations in the English-speaking world – one very close to Bath and the second the other side of the Irish Sea – that can also claim to be the origin of 'pay on the nail' or 'cash on the nail'. One is in Bristol, which still has four 'nails' outside its former Corn Exchange, now St Nicholas Market, the oldest of which is undated but believed to be from the late 1500s. The other is located in Limerick, whose Civic Museum contains a nail from 1685 that was once located in their former Exchange on Nicholas Street.

But are you at sixes and sevens as to the meaning of 'on the nail'? Let's not beat about the bush. The dictionary definition of 'paying on the nail' is to settle a bill or pay a debt immediately and without delay. One meaning of nail (possibly from medieval times) was a shallow vessel mounted on a stand, and business was concluded by payment into the vessel. You don't have to pay this way when buying nails from M&K Hardware in the market.

The 20 stalls within Guildhall Market are always worth a peruse. Selling everything from leather goods to lighting and second-hand books to sweets, the stallholders pride themselves on offering personal attention to every customer, in a space where trading has taken place for more than 800 years and where nothing will cost you an arm and a leg.

ADDRESS Guildhall Market, 33 High Street, BA2 4AW TIP Within the Guildhall is Bath Record Office, which holds historic material from the 14th century to the present day (www.batharchives.co.uk).

65 Pet Cemetery

Where faithful friends are laid to rest

'In remembrance of Tim, a little pal.' 'Our faithful pet Jack.' 'Beautiful loving Boy, sadly missed.' 'In loving memory of our Lulu.' 'Our mate Chum.'

These are just a few of the smallest gravestones in Bath, hidden in plain sight in the middle of Parade Gardens, that form one of England's oldest pet cemeteries. The owners of these pets clearly thought the world of their faithful companions and built some relatively elaborate graves for their much-missed furry friends. One theory is that the graves, of which the earliest is from 1908, were dug when Parade Gardens were once private and belonged to the houses on North Parade, whose residents could access the grounds via tunnels. It is intriguing to think of funeral processions taking place for departed dogs that might have solemnly made their way through these underground passages, with evidence of arched openings to the service areas beneath the homes still able to be seen at the southern edge of Parade Gardens. A set of steps into the gardens from North Parade are also now closed.

Parade Gardens was originally laid out as St James' Gardens to provide space for visitors to Bath. According to Historic England, when John Wood began to develop North and South Parades to the south of St James' Gardens in 1738, 'these achieved pre-eminence among the places of fashionable resort in the city'. Wood planned the gardens with a central circular lawn or bowling green but this scheme was not fully realised, although plans from the 18th and 19th centuries show much of the layout was done in accordance with his wishes, despite pets buried where the bowling green might have been.

The pet cemetery is a fascinating glimpse of the love for animals and tells the story of a Victorian fascination with death, the macabre and the afterlife; although Microdot, the last pet to be buried here, was laid to rest in 1988.

ADDRESS Parade Gardens, Grand Parade, BA2 4DF (what3words: skill.moving.office)
TIP Feeling in need of refreshment? A traditional lemonade stand operates in the summer on Grand Parade overlooking Parade Gardens. The choice is sweet, medium or sour.

66 Pétanque

Boules of steel

The most French of games has been adopted by Bathonians so much so that the clinking of metal balls hitting each other has become the sound of the city's summer. Another sound often heard during a game of pétanque (it's often mistakenly said that the name of the game is an onomatopoeia) is the popping of a bottle of something fizzy, ideally French of course. Because this is a sport that can be played with a glass in one hand and a boule in the other. The rules are simple: get your boule closer to the jack than your opponent.

Over the years, some famous names have played pétanque in Queen Square, which has several permanent *pistes* in the shadow of its obelisk. Joanna Lumley, Michael Palin and Terry Jones have all taken part in the annual Bath Boules tournament (www.bathboules.com), which began in the late 1980s as a one-day affair for restaurant staff across the city. The first event was the brainchild of Jean Pierre Auge of the former Le Beaujolais restaurant on Chapel Row and Philip Addis of Great Western Wine Company. It was an immediate success and dozens of teams now take part, with hundreds of thousands of pounds raised for charity. In 2026, the running of Bath Boules will be taken on by Bath Business Improvement District, hoping to grow the much-loved event even further. If you do decide to form a team, it's de rigueur to have a pun as your name. Previous participants have included I'm a Bouliever, Trestlemania and Aquae Boulis.

Get your training in before the next Bath Boules at the City of Bath Pétanque Club, which organises regular practice and open sessions at both their headquarters at Larkhall Sports Club and every Wednesday morning in Queen Square. Play for fun or take things more seriously (perhaps put that delicious glass of red wine in your hand down) in league matches against other clubs, or go on overseas tours to play international opposition.

ADDRESS City of Bath Pétanque Club, Larkhall Sports Club, Charlcombe Lane, BA1 8DJ, www.bathboules.co.uk TIP The Francis Hotel on the south side of Queen Square reopened in 2024 following a £14 million refurbishment. Its restaurant, Emberwood, specialises in fire-led cooking (www.francishotel.com).

67 Plasticine

How a Bath teacher invented a worldwide phenomenon

We've all probably played with Plasticine. Down the road in Bristol, the team at Aardman even have a collection of Oscar statuettes for their claymation creations. But neither Wallace nor Gromit nor any other much-loved characters would exist if it were not for a teacher from Bath who invented a worldwide phenomenon.

In 1897, William Harbutt, the head of Bath Art School, created a non-drying modelling clay made from clay, chalk, fatty acids and petroleum jelly. Like many of the best inventions, it was a solution to a problem: in Harbutt's case, to allow students to alter their sculptures during class. Patented in 1899, its commercial success came from a number of different reasons, including the fact that it was softer and more malleable than existing clays, which made it much easier for children to make models. Harbutt's new material also had the pleasing benefit of being non-toxic, unlike some other modelling materials from the time.

Harbutt called his invention Plasticine due to its plasticity. Manufacturing soon moved from the family home on Alfred Street to a former flour mill in Bathampton, where it could be made on an industrial scale. In World War I, the firm's chief modeller made models of German positions for the British Army. Harbutt and his wife Bessie commissioned artist friends to design different packaging, with the factory remaining in Bathampton until 1983.

There is a bust of Harbutt on the first floor of Victoria Art Gallery (www.victoriagal.org.uk). Before being cast in bronze, it was first modelled in Plasticine by one of Harbutt's own students, C. Whitney Smith. There is also a plaque praising Plasticine on Ye Grange on Bathampton High Street (a building that dates back to 1661). A nearby cul-de-sac is named Harbutts after the company that made Plasticine in Bath, to be enjoyed by children across the world.

ADDRESS Ye Grange, High Street, Bathampton, BA2 6SY TIP Find Plasticine and much more at the beautiful My Small World toy shop on St Lawrence Street within SouthGate shopping centre (www.mysmallworld.co.uk).

68 Pope's Walk

Ramblers, robbers and rhymes

Pope's Walk has been known throughout history as Hangman's Lane, Hanging Land Lane and Blind Lane, and is reputed to be haunted by a headless or blind horseman. It could also have been named because trees overhang the route, making this a wonderfully picturesque spot. Hanging land means 'land on a slope' so the thoroughfare's unusual former moniker is likely to be more prosaic than paranormal. The evocative lane may not have ghosts and ghouls along its length, but it still has an atmospheric – some may say spooky – feeling, particularly after dark. One story is that highwaymen and thieves used to lurk here to attack unsuspecting passers-by but these days you will find more ramblers than robbers.

Its current name comes from Alexander Pope (1688–1744), who as well as his poetry, satire and essays, is also credited with helping in the creation of Prior Park Landscape Garden, advising his friend Ralph Allen on its design. Prior Park contains within its grounds one of only four Palladian bridges in the world and the bridge across Pope's Walk, alternatively known as the Dry Arch or Rustic Arch, was built to carry one of the carriageways that Allen had built around his estate. (The horseman mentioned above could have lost his head while riding under this tunnel-like structure or a gust of wind caught his cloak on its stones, causing him to be hanged.)

Regardless of what you call it and whether you believe you will encounter any ghosts, Pope's Walk is an ancient route into the centre of Bath from the village of Combe Down. Look out for a boundary stone marking the border between Combe Down and Lyncombe and Widcombe. In Saxon times, it was here that there might have been a moot tree that was once central to local democracy. This was a place, often on a hill, where assemblies – known as moots – were held, important decisions made and justice dished out.

ADDRESS Pope's Walk, BA2 5AY TIP Close to the bottom of Pope's Walk is Perrymead Cemetery, which contains the sumptuously decorated Eyre Chantry, a mortuary chapel for the Eyre family dating from 1860.

69 Prince of Orange Obelisk

Bowling, bathing and tulips

Once part of the churchyard of Bath Priory and later used as a bowling green, the space around the Prince of Orange Obelisk in the middle of Orange Grove was named Alkmaar Garden following the end of World War II. Its moniker comes from Bath's twin city in the Netherlands. A major fundraising effort to send thousands of items of clothing to Alkmaar was inspired by an Alkmaar evacuee, Elias Prins, a playwright, theatre producer and activist who made his home in Bath after escaping from the Netherlands on a small fishing boat. Prins was a vocal anti-Nazi in the lead-up to the war and a secret helper of Jews seeking to leave Germany. In his new home in England, the Nazis were back and Prins served as an air raid warden during the bombing of Bath in 1942. In 1946, the people of Alkmaar gave 5,000 tulip bulbs to be planted in Alkmaar Garden, and to mark the 80th anniversary of the twinning agreement in 2025, 24,000 bulbs were donated and planted in locations across the city.

The obelisk itself also has a Dutch link. It commemorates the successful cure of the Prince of Orange in 1734 following his visit to Bath. In the same year, the prince, who later became William IV of the Netherlands, married Anne, the eldest daughter of Britain's King George II. Paid for by Beau Nash, the obelisk was both a monument and a 30 foot (9 metre)-high advertisement. In the words of John Wood, it acted as 'no small recommendation to the building material of the hills of Bath for such sort of ornaments'.

If you like obelisks, you're in the right city. The obelisk occupying a prime position at the centre of Queen Square was erected in 1738 in honour of Frederick, Prince of Wales, and originally stood within a basin of water. A third obelisk goes by the name of the Victoria Column, unveiled at the entrance to Royal Victoria Park by the 11-year-old Princess Victoria in 1830.

ADDRESS Alkmaar Garden, Orange Grove, BA1 1LP TIP Browns on Orange Grove is located within Bath's former police station. The cells are now the restaurant's toilets (www.browns-restaurants.co.uk).

70 Pulteney Radial Gate

An essential piece of urban infrastructure

The weir in front of Pulteney Bridge might feature on all of the post-cards and Instagram reels, but look next to it to find the real star of the show. Pulteney Radial Gate was built at the same time as the three-tiered horseshoe-shaped weir. Some may view it as an eyesore, constantly clogged with branches, but this is an essential piece of urban infrastructure, without which Bath would be constantly under threat of being underwater. Both the radial gate and the weir were constructed following floods in the 1960s. The gate's special skill is that it automatically adapts to changing water flows to maintain river levels upstream while also allowing flood flows through.

A plaque on one side of the sluice erected by the Bristol Avon River Flood Authority – the now extinct body responsible for the Bath Flood Protection Scheme – commemorates its opening on 2 June 1972, confusingly by the lord mayor of London. The plaque remembers the chief engineer, Frank Greenhalgh, also in charge of the Twerton Gates at the downstream end. These gates span across the width of the Avon, maintaining a constant water level under normal low-flow conditions but raising during floods.

In 2025, plans were being discussed by local politicians and the Environment Agency to replace the gate with a small hydroelectric scheme to generate power for nearby buildings including the Guildhall, Guildhall Market, Victoria Art Gallery, and Bath Sports & Leisure Centre and its heated pool. North Somerset Council have called their plans – part of a commitment for the council's estate to be carbon neutral by 2030 – 'the most exciting and ambitious inner-city hydro-electric project in Europe'. These plans are more likely to go ahead than an aborted project from 1973, just a year after the weir and radial gate were opened, which invited tenders for a pub or restaurant to be built on top of the gate.

ADDRESS Spring Gardens Road, BA2 4BQ, +44 (0)1225 464429 **TIP** Pulteney Cruisers leave from between the radial gate and Pulteney Bridge. The one-hour tours on double-decker boats head up the River Avon to the village of Bathampton and back (www.pulteneycruisers.com).

71 Ralph Allen's Town House

Almost completely hidden from view

To see and be seen was among the main preoccupations of the fashionable residents of Georgian Bath. What was the point of living in one of the city's most splendid homes if nobody could see that you lived there? Ralph Allen – a man instrumental in Bath's prominence – therefore would probably have been bitterly disappointed to find out that the town house that still retains his name is now almost completely hidden from view. Allen had become Bath's postmaster at the age of just 19, later improving postal routes across England and using his new-found wealth to buy quarries at Combe Down and Bathampton Down, whose Bath stone was used to build the city.

There are two ways to see Ralph Allen's Town House. The best unobstructed view is revealed by walking into Topping & Co. bookshop and then finding a door down a short flight of stairs that takes you to a small outside courtyard. Opening up in front of you from this vantage point is the house (most recently used as offices) in all of its glory. If Topping is closed, then you will have to make do with a slightly obstructed side view from York Street, with the house able to be glimpsed through a small gap between the bookshop and an ice cream parlour.

It was not always like this, however, and the elaborate façade of Ralph Allen's Town House was originally designed by John Wood the Elder in around 1727 to be very much seen – until it was hidden by changes to the road layout as the city developed around the building. This was Allen's home and the commonly heard story is that he had the Sham Castle built to improve the view from the house that later became his offices when he moved to Prior Park in 1745.

Pevsner's Architectural Guide to Bath describes the 'oddly tall and narrow building' as akin to 'a miniature Roman temple'. Look out for Corinthian columns, a decorated pediment and richly carved garlands with fruits and flowers.

ADDRESS York Street, BA1 1NG TIP Prior Park and its landscape garden is a National Trust property on Ralph Allen Drive, with one of only four Palladian bridges found in the world (www.nationaltrust.org.uk/visit/bath-bristol/prior-park-landscape-garden).

72 Real Tennis

The sport of kings

Burn marks from a fire in 1937 are visible on a beam in the shop at the Museum of Bath at Work. Back then, both washing powder and floor polish were made in this building that had a very lucky escape from being completely destroyed. Over the years, it has been a drill hall, boxing venue, circus, school, venue for political rallies and typewriter case manufacturer, before opening in 1978 as a museum dedicated to Bath's industrial history. For our purposes, however, we will be travelling back in time to 1777 when the building opened as a real tennis court.

King Henry VIII is the most famous real tennis player, with the modern game of tennis developing from this indoor sport, which is a mixture of tennis and squash. (Real tennis also shares many similarities with the rapidly growing sport of padel. A headline in the *Daily Mail* in 2025 screamed that Bath was 'waging a war' against the sport, claiming [incorrectly] that the city 'has banned the popular racket sport completely because well-heeled residents say sound of games is "Chinese water torture"'. Never let facts get in the way of a good story.) The world's most famous real tennis court at Hampton Court Palace in London was built for Cardinal Wolsey between 1526 and 1529. The court at Hampton Court still played on today dates back to 1625 and the game continued to be popular 150 years later when Bath's real tennis court was constructed – a rare example of a Georgian-period court.

Richard Scrace, the optimistic entrepreneur who also ran a neighbouring horse-riding school, borrowed the equivalent of more than £1 million today to build his real tennis court in Bath, perhaps thinking that like today's padel craze he would have a licence to print money. But he was unable to repay a hefty mortgage and he put the building up for sale after only eight months, after which it took on a number of surprising uses.

ADDRESS Museum of Bath at Work, Julian Road, BA1 2RH, +44 (0)1225 318348, www.museumofbath.org TIP Next door to the Museum of Bath at Work is Christ Church, which opened in 1798 as a 'preaching house'. Choral Evensong is usually held here on the third Sunday of the month.

73 Rebecca Fountain

'Water is best'

The marble statue of Rebecca outside Bath Abbey was erected at a time when a growing movement attempted to steer the citizenry away from the evils of alcohol. For the avoidance of doubt as to its purpose, two inscriptions encircle its base: *Take the water of life freely* and *Water is best*. An organisation called the Bath Temperance Association was behind this particular statue, now Grade II-listed, which was designed by Rushton Walker and erected in 1861. The fountain has not worked for many years but the statue remains a popular meeting point for Bathonians.

Bath Temperance Association ceased to exist in 2000 but was once just one of similar groups up and down the country who left behind not just fountains but also temperance halls, coffee houses and hotels as Victorian England battled for self-improvement and total abstinence. The temperance movement was linked to the Metropolitan Drinking Fountain & Cattle Trough Association, who campaigned for free clean drinking water and better animal welfare.

The choice of Rebecca as the woman depicted in the statue comes from Rebecca, or Rebekah, in Genesis, indicating how the temperance movement was closely linked with Christianity. She was the wife of Isaac and the mother of twins Esau and Jacob. In the story told in the first book of the Old Testament in the Bible, we meet Rebecca by the well, where she had come to draw water.

Sadly, in 2025, the Rebecca Fountain was damaged by vandals who yanked the bowl upwards, exposing the pins that hold it on top of the column. It was not the first vandalism either, with damage also occurring in 2004 and 2022, meaning that minor repairs had to be made. The latest repairs saw the area around the statue fenced off and a team from Cliveden Conservation fixing the stonework, and using the opportunity to also clean the marble statue and its sandstone base.

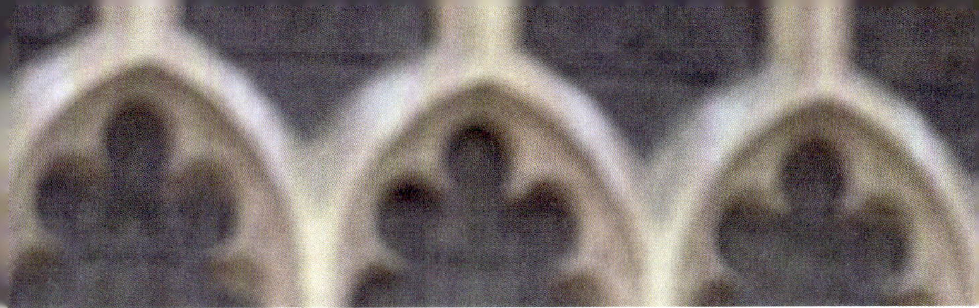

ADDRESS Kingston Parade, BA1 5EB **TIP** If temperance isn't your thing, close to the fountain on the corner of Cheap Street and High Street is The Whisky Shop (www.whiskyshop.com).

74 The Rec Turnstiles

Edwardian sporting elegance

When proposals for Bath Rugby's new stadium at the Recreation Ground were revealed in 2023, an architectural firm specialising in classical and traditional design came up with an audacious alternative. Rather than 'wrecking the Rec' with a stadium 'at odds with Bath's animated roofscape', Apollodorus Architecture's counter-proposal (www.apollodorus.uk/project-bath-arena) was for a Colosseum-like structure inspired by the city's Roman heritage. Its proponents might never have truly believed that their dream would become a reality but this was both a theoretical exercise and a provocation seeking to spark conversations. 'Counter projects come into being when a special place is so blighted or threatened that those who love it, be they architects, urban designers or community groups, can no longer stand by in frustration and impotence but feel compelled to envision something better,' says the Apollodorus team.

In 2025, Bath & North East Somerset Council approved Bath Rugby's planning application for a new 18,000-seater stadium at the Rec. It may be more rectangular than Roman but at least it keeps the club at their historic home.

The beginnings of what is now Bath Rugby – one of England's most successful teams – can be traced back to 1865. For their first three decades, the team was an itinerant one, playing matches at Claverton Down, Kensington Meadows, North Parade, Lambridge Meadows and Henrietta Park. Their first game at the Rec was played against Exeter in 1894. The pair of wooden turnstiles with ogee crested roofs at the entrance to the Rec at the end of William Street were built around a year later, granting Edwardian rugby fans access to what was then still known as Pulteney Meadows and used to regularly flood. Rugby remains at the heart of Bath and a match day cheering on the modern-day gladiators has to be experienced by any sports fan.

ADDRESS Pulteney Mews, BA2 4DS **TIP** The Rotary Club of Bath hosts an annual fireworks display at the Recreation Ground, with all proceeds going to charity (www.rotarybath.org.uk).

75 RoadPeace Memorial

Remembering lives lost on the road

RoadPeace closed as a charity in 2026 but their work lives on in a memorial within a small park in Bath. The organisation offered support for road crash victims and their families for more than 30 years, with the RoadPeace Memorial in Pigeon Park bearing the inscription, *Remembering lives lost and broken on our roads in the South West.*

Bath's RoadPeace Memorial was designed by Rebecca Yeo and carved from Bath stone by the sculptor Yannick Li-Ah-Kane. It was unveiled in 2010 at a ceremony attended by more than 100 people, including MP Dan Foster and representatives from the police, fire service and local authority. Musical accompaniment came from the Bathwick Church Choir, and seven doves were released, symbolising the seven counties across the South West region and the average number of people who were then killed on Britain's roads every day. The RoadPeace logo of a dove is on the memorial within a circle of black marble, underneath which are ivy leaves.

Before they closed, RoadPeace erected smaller memorials at the places where people died. They also took part in campaigns, including for stronger sentences for motorists who have caused death by dangerous driving, and calling for the word 'accident' not to be used when talking about crashes. More than twice as many people are killed on the UK's roads each year than as a result of murder and terrorism combined.

Pigeon Park, in which Bath's RoadPeace Memorial can be found, is located between Lower Borough Walls and St James's Parade. It's a peaceful spot on the site of the original city walls next to the Chapel Arts Centre. Formerly a burial ground, its official name is St James Park but its nickname is the one that has stuck. Where some say witches were once burned at the stake, it is now a spot where our feathered friends flock to, joining office workers for lunch on a sunny day.

ADDRESS Pigeon Park, BA1 1QR TIP In the grounds of St Martin's Hospital on Midford Road is a memorial to US rock&roll legend Eddie Cochran, who died there in 1960 aged just 21 the day after a car crash.

76 Roundhill Monument

A mysterious ancient meeting point

Twerton Roundhill is believed to be a religious site of Bath's water goddess, Sulis Minerva. But you wouldn't know that if visiting today. The cast gold face of Sulis Minerva on display in the Roman Baths is one of the city's most famous historic artefacts, holding its own against any Roman antiquity discovered anywhere else in the world. Don't expect a similar treasure here unless what floats your boat is a stone stump usually covered in graffiti scrawls. But there most definitely is still a wow factor in the views afforded from this spot across huge swathes of Somerset countryside and even as far as Wales on a particularly clear day, with a panoramic vista of the city stretching out the other way. Bath has many wonderful viewpoints but this could well be the best. Watch glorious sunsets or join astronomers after dark to glimpse even more distant views.

On the edge of the city, this higher ground is one of a series of natural roundhills which, millions of years ago, were formed from harder rock than the land around it. As well as being thought to have been a religious site for the Romans, it could also have been used later by the Saxons as a meeting point and ceremonial place. Today this is a wildflower-rich local nature reserve on what was once ancient woodland.

A website called Waters of the Gap (www.watersofthegap.com) documents a visit to Roundhill during an intriguing project based on the legends surrounding Sulis Minerva. Dylan Spicer imagines if the goddess had appeared on the hill, 'framed by the glow of the sun', in a place that he says could be 'the key to cracking the mystery'. He writes, 'The goddess of the water is also the goddess in the sun in much of our reading. Is Roundhill the place that joins them together? Is this hidden corner of Bath an often forgotten monument to its geology? We strolled back down the hill to reality'.

ADDRESS Roundhill, Wedmore Close, BA2 1LG TIP A roundhill in Kelston was an ancient burial site. Kelston Roundhill Walk is part of the Cotswold Way, one of Britain's most popular walking trails (www.cotswoldwayassociation.org.uk).

77 St Ann's Place

Saved from the wrecking ball

Looking at St Ann's Place now, it is impossible to imagine that this was once on the front line of a battle to save the very soul of Bath. Built in the 1770s, St Ann's Place is a small and narrow cul-de-sac, with houses on three sides looking onto a stone-flagged courtyard. Today, it is typical of the city's world-famous Georgian character but may well have been brutally bulldozed if council officials in the 1960s and 1970s had got their way.

A photograph of St Ann's Place with broken windows and cracked roof tiles features in a 1973 book, *The Sack of Bath* by Adam Fergusson. His book is based on a series of articles he wrote for *The Times* about the public anger against the council's plans to demolish large swathes of artisan housing across the city. Its publishers Persephone Books call it 'a fierce and angry polemic. Through words and photographs it is unashamedly outspoken, outraged and vituperative.' The book and its photographs, some by Lord Snowdon, are credited with helping to halt headlong destruction and saving many much-loved corners of the city from the wrecking ball.

In the preface to a new edition of the book published in 1989, Fergusson wrote: '*The Sack of Bath* was the product of the collective cultural blindness of those who ran Bath four decades ago, and of the simmering, bursting indignation of those who cared about it… *The Sack of Bath*'s publication in 1973 was the culmination of an already prolonged effort to lever the progressive destruction of Bath's Georgian character into the popular consciousness. If it came too late to save much, it was in time to save a great deal more.'

Historic England call numbers 5, 6 and 7 St Ann's Place 'a notable survival of artisanal housing, laid out around a close'. This trio of homes was fully restored in the early 1980s by architect Aaron Evans, just a decade after their possible demolition.

ADDRESS St Ann's Place, BA1 2BJ TIP Percy Community Centre on New King Street hosts a large number of classes and activities for all ages (www.percycentre.org.uk).

78 St John's Foundation

Nine centuries of charity

In a city with a proud and illustrious history, a charity that continues to function more than 850 years after its formation deserves to be celebrated. St John's Foundation did indeed mark its 850th anniversary in 2024 with a year of celebration and a special event in Bath Abbey. Be sure to put 2174 in your diary, because then it will be 1,000 years since French cleric Bishop Reginald Fitzjocelyn created St John's Hospital to alleviate poverty and chronic living conditions in Bath.

Much has changed since the establishment of this medieval refuge, which provided food and shelter for the poor. But nine centuries later, the St John's of today still provides accommodation and support. This includes the provision of housing for older adults, as well as outreach services that help people to live independently for longer.

Dating back to 1444 and rebuilt in 1553, St Catherine's Hospital on Bilbury Lane next to Thermae Bath Spa was originally an almshouse, which has been transformed into 10 luxury apartments for short stays (st-catherines-hospital.guestybookings.com), generating funding for St John's charitable work. Also a modern source of income is the House of St John's (www.hosj.co.uk) on Queen Square, gifted to the charity in 1953 by the Whittington family (descendants of Dick Whittington), which is now a work and event space.

The Chapel of St Michael's Within in Chapel Court is also part of the St John's estate and is open every day, either as a place for quiet reflection or just for looking around. The first Norman chapel here was dedicated to St John the Baptist but rededicated to St Michael when the original St Michael's Within (so called because it was within the medieval city walls) fell into disrepair in the 19th century. Look out for the timber bell tower built around 1580 and the clock on the eastern gable, one of Bath's earliest public clocks.

ADDRESS St John's Foundation, 4–5 Chapel Court, BA1 1SQ, www.stjohnsbath.org.uk
TIP The Gainsborough Bath Spa on Beau Street is a five-star hotel owned by the same people as Thermae Bath Spa. The hotel's spa is the only one in the UK to use natural thermal waters (www.thegainsboroughbathspa.co.uk).

79 Sedan Chair Lodges

The only surviving structures of their kind

Spare a thought for Bath's sedan chairmen, who spent every day on their feet, ferrying customers across a city that has a number of exceedingly steep hills and, due to its status as a health resort, a higher than average number of people who would not have been able to walk. But even those in perfect health would also have made use of the chairs, enabling passengers to not just be carried by either two or four chairmen (depending on their weight) through narrow streets but also inside one building to another, or even straight into the baths.

Two buildings on Queen's Parade are unique in the UK as previously being sedan chair lodges. Located to the rear of 24 Queen Square, they date from the 1730s and were built as places where chairmen were able to rest between trips.

Chairmen were not officially licensed in Bath until 1708, when they had to pay an annual fee to the Corporation of three shillings and carry a distinguishing mark or number. Fares were set at sixpence for any transit within the walls, one shilling for any journey from inside the walls to St James' or St Michael's parishes, and up to sixpence for every half hour of waiting. Fines could be dished out for overcharging, swearing or refusing to carry a passenger.

Trevor Fawcett from the History of Bath Research Group paints an evocative picture of Bath in the sedan chair era: 'Passengers had to trust to the chairmen's competence, surefootedness, and skill in synchronising their pace and manoeuvres. Occasionally there were accidents: a chairman stumbled or ran into something, windows shattered, the whole contraption overturned. Sedanmen often showed scant respect for pedestrians even on pavements, demanding precedence and the near side of buildings, taking corners too fast, and jostling through constricted areas like the notorious narrow passage between Orange Grove and Terrace Walk.'

ADDRESS Queen's Parade Place, BA1 2NN TIP Sedan Chair House West is the headquarters of Hawker Joinery, with a sedan chair parked permanently outside (www.hawker-joinery.co.uk).

80 Shakespeare's Monument

'We shall not look on his like again'

A monument to commemorate the 300th anniversary of William Shakespeare's birth was erected in Royal Victoria Gardens in 1864. On it is an inscription with quotes from *Coriolanus* and *Hamlet*: *Tongues speak. This was a man. Take him for all in all. We shall not look on his like again.*

Bath being Bath, the monument is in the form of a Roman altar, 'remarkably classical given its subject', according to Historic England. It was one of the first works of city surveyor Charles Davis, self-styled as Major Davis following a stint in the army, who helped change the face of his home city where he lived his whole life and was usually seen with his beloved deerhounds by his side. Davis has been called 'a solid but controversial pillar of the Victorian establishment'. Many of his buildings still stand today, including the Ladymead Fountain on Walcot Street, the former police station on Orange Grove and, the most spectacular of the lot, Grand Parade and the Empire Hotel with its curious gables in three different styles, rising up from the colonnade below which was a firing range during World War II.

Davis can also be credited with the rediscovery in 1880 of the original Roman baths, buried in silt under the later baths built in the 12th and 16th centuries. Numerous conflicts, however, meant that he was not able to fulfil his plans of building a roof over the baths. There might have even been some skulduggery involved too, with Davis winning a scheme put out to an anonymous open competition, but forgetting to put his contact details on the envelope submitted with his designs and his win therefore being recommended to be discarded.

Davis was also a keen archaeologist and antiquarian, with the cross on his grave in Smallcombe Garden Cemetery a replica of the Saxon one that he helped discover during excavations beneath Bath Abbey.

ADDRESS Royal Victoria Park, BA1 2LZ TIP In nearby Frome are two surviving pillars of four entrance gate piers designed by Charles Davis as part of a scheme for a grand crescent to rival Bath's Royal Crescent.

81 Sham Castle

Built as an 'eyecatcher' – or was it?

Read most of the literature about Sham Castle and you will learn that Ralph Allen built it to enhance the view from his town house now tucked behind Toppings bookshop. But in 2025, Mike Macklin gave a talk at the Bath Royal Literary & Scientific Institution in which he speculated that this was not the case.

The tale that Sham Castle was constructed as an 'eyecatcher' has been repeated so many times over the years that it is accepted as the truth. What is undisputed is that the structure was erected in around 1762 on land previously occupied by a rabbit warren. What appears to be a castle from afar is in fact only one wall. It's a sham, although there was also a field nearby called Sham Down before the building of Sham Castle, so it is both a sham castle and Sham Castle.

'All the information tends to be ambiguous, contradictory and confusing,' Macklin told his audience in the talk that can be watched on YouTube. Nevertheless, he presents a compelling and well-researched argument that Sham Castle was never meant to be an eyecatcher from Ralph Allen's Town House; not least because Allen himself had moved to the spectacular Prior Park by the time Sham Castle had been built and would have had plenty to look out on from that palatial home. Another major problem with the most common story is that Sham Castle would also have been impossible to see from the house when the castle was constructed due to buildings surrounding it. And neither does it directly face the house, being positioned instead towards the end of London Road.

'I think what we've got is a charming but erroneous tale which through constant repetition has become accepted fact,' Macklin says when concluding his talk. 'What we have is Ralph Allen doing something for everybody rather than for his own personal gain and something that everybody can enjoy.'

ADDRESS Golf Course Road, BA2 6JG TIP Founded in 1880, Bath Golf Club is known colloquially as the Sham Castle and uses the structure as its logo (www.bathgolfclub.org.uk).

82 Shree Jagannatha Temple

A spiritual haven

People come from all over the world to visit the only Hindu temple in Europe dedicated to Maha Prabhu Shree Jagannatha. But this temple on the outskirts of Bath is on borrowed time in its current location.

In the Hindu belief, Shree Jagannatha is omnipresent, omnipotent and omniscient. He is also known as Parameshwara (supreme lord), Param-Brahman (supreme omnipresent god) and Paramatma (supreme self). His most elaborate temple in Puri in Odisha on the east coast of India is just one where devotees pray to him to remove sin and give salvation. This temple was founded in the 12th century and is dedicated to Lord Jagannatha and his siblings Balabhadra and Subhadra.

So how did a small temple to this deity end up in Bath? Among the challenges of the pandemic, the temple is a testament to the faith of its founders, many of whom are from the Odia diaspora with a particularly close connection to Shree Jagannatha.

The story begins in January 2020 when two Odia filmmakers, Ajit Nanda and Parshuram Patri, visited the UK. Their visit laid the groundwork for the foundation of a community interest company (CIC) founded by Arun Kar, Susmit Nayak and Pratap Prusty. Bath's Hindu community then came to the fore and Ashish Rajhansha and Susmita Rajhansha joined the CIC. Premises in Bath were located and deities were meticulously crafted in Puri, undergoing a parikrama (circumambulation) of the main temple in Puri, before being taken to Ahmedabad and New Delhi for more religious ceremonies, then arriving in London and finally in Bath.

The Shree Jagannatha Temple opened in 2021 in part of the former Culverhay School, with this location always meant to be temporary until a permanent temple could be built. So for now the temple is here but there are plans for Bath & North East Somerset Council to demolish the current buildings to make way for two new schools.

ADDRESS Rush Hill, BA2 2QH, +44 (0)1225 941103, www.shreejagannathatemple.org.uk
TIP Bath Mosque is located within a former house on 8 Pierrepont Street with two Jumu'ah prayers held every Friday (www.bathmosque.org.uk).

83 Sir Bevil Grenville's Monument

Commemorating a commander and his Cornish pikemen

'It is difficult today to imagine the horror of the Civil War battle that took place on this spot,' says English Heritage's description of Sir Bevil Grenville's Monument. Topped by a gryphon, it stands on the battlefield of Lansdown Hill, marking the centre of a Royalist attack on the Parliamentary army's position in July 1643. The battle ended in a stalemate but led to the death of Grenville, a Royalist colonel who was killed while gallantly leading his Cornish pikemen.

Examine the monument built in the early 18th century and you will see Grenville's name has once been misspelled as 'Granville' – but this is still a grand reminder to the commander. Also on the monument is a poem about the death of Grenville by William Cartwright, a fellow Royalist who also died in 1643: *This was not Nature's courage nor that thing / We valour call which Time and Reason bring / But a diviner fury fierce and high / Valour transported into Ecstasy.*

When the English Civil War broke out, King Charles I had no professional army. Instead, noblemen such as Grenville called upon his tenants to fight for their favoured side. Alongside fellow Cornish squires, Sir Nicholas Slanning, John Trevanion and John Arundel, Grenville helped to raise a force of more than 1,500 infantrymen who became the nucleus of the king's army in the West Country.

At the top of Lansdown Hill, Parliamentarian forces under Sir William Waller attempted to prevent two Royalist armies from joining together. It was here where Grenville and his Cornish infantry began fighting their way up the steep slopes to attack Waller's guns. In an almost suicidal act of bravery, the Cornish troops succeeded in their third attempt to take the guns but Grenville was then killed in a counter-attack.

ADDRESS Battlefields, BA1 9DD, www.english-heritage.org.uk/visit/places/sir-bevil-grenvilles-monument **TIP** As well as horse racing, Bath Racecourse on Lansdown Hill holds a number of special events throughout the year (www.bath-racecourse.co.uk).

84 Slippery Lane

An ancient thoroughfare

You can no longer slip or slide down Slippery Lane because it is closed off at the top. It may be inaccessible today but you can still look down this narrow thoroughfare that once provided access to the River Avon just outside the city walls. The dark passageway gives an evocative indication of what it would have been like to live in Bath during the Middle Ages.

Following the fall of the Roman Empire, Bath's most famous former residents departed from the urban centre but it is likely that the site was not entirely abandoned. By 675 there was a convent of nuns in Bath and around 880 a new street layout took shape that is still recognisable today. Edgar was crowned King of England in Bath in 973 and by the completion of the Domesday Book in 1086, Bath had a population of at least 1,000 residents. By the 13th century, Bath had a well-developed cloth trade and this remained important until the early 16th century. The Black Death in the mid-14th century most likely decimated Bath's population, with between 300 and 600 adults living here by 1381. Just over two centuries later in 1590, Bath's city status was conferred by royal charter.

The perilous detritus being washed out from butchers and fishmongers along Slippery Lane is believed to be the reason for its unusual moniker, in place from at least 1777. Look closely and you will be able to see bricked-up doorways which, like Eastgate, show the original street level of Bath.

Also known as Northgate Lane, another former name of Slippery Lane could have been Ducking Stool Lane as at its end was where Bath's ducking stool was located. In use across England by the 17th century, this cruel form of punishment saw a person – most often a woman – strapped onto a chair attached to a wooden beam and repeatedly ducked into the water, often causing death by shock or drowning.

ADDRESS Off Northgate Street, BA1 5AS TIP Walk down Podium Terrace above where Slippery Lane would have once come out at the River Avon to enjoy the less-observed back view of Pulteney Bridge.

85 Smallcombe Cemetery

Rescued from decay by the community

It wouldn't be a cemetery in Bath if it weren't perched on the side of a hill offering views far across the city. Smallcombe Garden Cemetery is located at the end of what was once a sweeping carriage drive that has seen better days. The same could be said for a few corners of this cemetery, some of whose graves are hidden among overgrown foliage. Footpaths wind up the steep banks, making their way through bushes obscuring graves. But much of Smallcombe Garden Cemetery is also very well cared for with the grass in pristine condition. This former meadow on the edge of a small wood might all be overgrown by now if not for the actions of the local community. No further plots were available here after 1988 and the cemetery became neglected before funds were raised for its sensitive restoration from 2014.

Smallcombe Garden Cemetery may be viewed as one cemetery but there are in fact two separate cemeteries here divided by a wall to the right of the entrance gate. The first cemetery opened when St Mary's churchyard in Bathwick became full. Its chapel dating from 1855 is an early work by architect Thomas Fuller, who later designed the Canadian parliament buildings. The other side of the dividing wall is the non-conformist section, with its octagonal chapel built in 1861 by Alfred Goodridge.

Venture up one of the slopes and you will find a bench in memory of Neil Susan Curse (1944–2013) with the words: *At rest with a view of Bath to share with family and friends.* The bench itself is just about accessible and also provides a view of cows in a neighbouring field; but look to the left while seated on it and you can see a few graves being consumed by foliage. Among some of the more well-known men and women buried here, let's remember Charles Edward Shaw, who died in 1901 aged just four months, his small headstone a reminder of his tragically young age.

ADDRESS Widcombe Hill, BA2 6DD, www.smallcombegardencemetery.org
TIP Smallcombe Nuttery off Horseshoe Walk is a project from Transition Bath. The nuts and berries are grown for community use, with anyone invited to take a fair share when they are ripe (www.transitionbath.org).

86 South Lodge Gates

'Pastiche but of the very highest order'

Bath is not a big place. According to the latest census data, there are 75 English towns and cities in England with bigger populations, including Watford, Maidstone and Oldham. Bath may only have around 94,000 residents but it has more than 5,000 listed buildings, structures and monuments. Walk around the city for only a short time and you will appreciate why it has one of the highest concentrations of listed buildings in the country.

But the historic significance of Bath, and its proliferation of listed buildings and conservation areas – as well as the extra status of being a UNESCO World Heritage Site – can cause problems. An act of parliament legally protects all listed buildings from inappropriate development that would harm their character as a 'building of special architectural or historic interest'. If you want to make any changes to a listed building either inside and out, front and back, you must gain the required consent. Bath even has its own specific guidance put together by the Bath Preservation Trust (www.bath-preservation-trust.org.uk) in order to help owners of listed buildings looking to repair, extend, alter or change their properties.

As mentioned above, it is not just buildings that feature on Historic England's list but also a number of different structures, which can include just about anything. On Sion Hill, a collection of cast iron gates, gate piers and railings dating from the mid-20th century have held Grade II listed status since 1972. Historic England's listing says the 'elaborate screen of gates and railings... produced a prestigious and extremely secluded development'. They are further described as an 'outstanding ensemble of Regency-style cast iron street furniture... constructed to serve as the entrance screen to Ernest Cook's embellishment of Summerhill, Sion Hill Place. As such, the ensemble is pastiche but of the very highest order'.

ADDRESS Sion Hill, BA1 2UQ TIP The raised pavement and railings fronting nearby Cavendish Crescent are also Grade II listed.

87 Splasherist

Mess not minimalism

The definition of 'rage painting' according to the Urban Dictionary is choosing to paint when you are extremely angry. It doesn't matter what you are mad about. 'You blast your favourite music at full volume and just let your hands, brush or anything else you paint with do the work for you.' At Splasherist, these painting implements include bottles, sponges and tennis balls – all to help you create your unique canvas at this first-of-its-kind experience in the UK. You will be given protective clothing and goggles to wear too because this is certainly not minimalism. The layers of paint on the walls, floor and ceiling around you tell the story of previous participants and your pristine white canvas will not stay blank for long as your painting session begins and the paint starts to fly.

You certainly don't have to be raging to have fun at Splasherist, which opened on Widcombe Parade in 2023 and now has two sister venues. Get messy as you de-stress while channelling Jackson Pollock, who popularised what became known as the 'drip technique' from 1947 to 1950. He covered the entire canvas with paint and you can do the same here, although dancing in Pollock's frenetic style is optional.

The sessions are meant to be cathartic experiences, with up to 16 people able to take part at the same time. Choose your non-toxic and water-based paints (with the addition of speciality paints if desired including glitter, metallic and neon options), choose your implements, and then spend 50 minutes in one of the Splasherist studios painting, splashing, flicking and throwing. Don't think too much about making a multi-million-pound masterpiece; just go freestyle. Once it has dried (which can take a few days depending on how much paint you have used), you can proudly display your unique canvas in your own home. A piece of art forever yours created in one of Bath's most bonkers businesses.

ADDRESS 12 Widcombe Parade, BA2 4JT, +44 (0)1225 596094, www.splasherist.com/bath-1 TIP Paint & Sip and Sculpt & Sip events take place at The Cork and the Pig & Fiddle (www.paintvine.co.uk).

88 Springfield Quarry

Once Bath's largest open quarry

The front cover of this book is an approximation of the colour of Bath stone. Walk through Springfield Quarry and on three sides you can see vertical walls that were once a site where this famous stone was excavated. These days, houses and back gardens cling to the top of the walls up to 10 metres (33 feet) high surrounding the former quarry that was once the largest open quarry in Bath. Quarrying had begun in this area by the 1720s, with mines previously extending in all directions from Combe Down village. Springfield Quarry operated from around 1750 to 1900 and, over its lifetime, yielded around 2.5 million cubic feet (around 125,000 tons) of stone. Bath stone may give Bath its unique feel but the stone was also used across the South West: including at Truro Cathedral, for 19th-century Weston-super-Mare, and for mansions at Tyntesfield and Gatcombe Park.

On a recent morning, a visitor to the quarry found a yellow golf ball – evidence of another new use for this land now designated as a Regionally Important Geological Site (RIGS). There is a surprising lack of signage nearby, with access only available via Entry Hill Park. On this cul-de-sac, the colours of the houses are the rich honey hue of this stone that gives Bath its distinctive glow.

Venture deeper into the former quarry along a muddy path and discover a small dell of trees. Graffiti tags sadly cover some of the former quarry walls, parts of which have been reinforced in order to hold up the houses above. From one angle, a home on Hawthorne Grove appears to rise vertically from these walls. Some hardy trees also make their home in the walls, defying gravity as they cling to the rock face. Find a blocked-up mine entrance on the eastern side and be sure not to venture too close to some sections that have been fenced off for safety, the sound of birdsong now replacing the sound of metal upon stone.

ADDRESS Springfield Quarry, BA2 5PH TIP Go straight to the source to enjoy the Choux Box Patisserie where their delicacies are made at Entry Hill (www.thechouxboxpatisserie.com).

89 The Story of Chocolate

When truth is stranger than fiction

Who was Charlotte Brunswick? According to a sign outside her eponymous shop on Church Street, Charlotte was 'the first and finest chocolatier in the city of Bath in the 18th century'. She was 'born into a family of explorers' who brought her home ingredients from their travels like cinnamon from China and oranges from Spain, and she used these to make chocolates 'so delicious and popular that Charlotte was soon renowned across the city of Bath'. Charlotte Brunswick Chocolates say that their recipes today 'are still inspired by her ideas and explorations'.

It's a lovely story but one that is completely made up. There is in fact a strong chocolate heritage in the West Country, but just down the road from Bath is Bristol where, in 1847, Fry's made the world's first mass-produced chocolate bar. Regardless of the elaborate story, the Charlotte Brunswick chocolates for sale are luxurious and presented in boxes that include a version of their very shop.

Sticking to fictional chocolatiers on your explorations of Bath, you might follow in the footsteps of Willy Wonka. In 2021, *Wonka*, starring Timothée Chalamet as the eccentric inventor, was filmed at locations across the city. Artificial snow appeared outside Bath Abbey, Parade Gardens were turned into a misty location, and more snow was added to the Colonnades, where Chalamet can be seen in an early scene sitting on a bench. Bath Street also provided another background and *Wonka* certainly is not the only film making the most of Bath's beauty. In 2012's *Les Misérables*, Pulteney Bridge stood in for 19th-century Paris; and Dyrham Park was used for the filming of the 1993 adaptation of *The Remains of the Day* starring Sir Anthony Hopkins. Another real-life film star, Nicolas Cage, turned on Bath's Christmas lights in 2009 after a local resident invited him by putting a letter through the door of his former home on The Circus.

ADDRESS 3 Church Street, BA1 1NL, +44 (0)1225 287669, www.charlottebrunswick.co.uk
TIP Chocoholics should also visit Mrs. Potts Chocolate House (www.mrspotts.co.uk) on York Street and Knoops (www.knoops.com) on Old Bond Street.

90 Suffragette Memorial

Remembering a 'nest of Suffragettes'

A solitary pine tree is all that remains of a former arboretum in Batheaston that commemorated the deeds of dozens of brave women. Eagle House was the country residence of the Blathwayt family, who offered their home as a place of recovery for women who were politically active as part of the Suffrage movement. The house became known as the 'Suffragettes' Retreat' and in 1909 one of the family, Emily Blathwayt, had the idea of encouraging everyone who stayed there to plant a tree in a field, which became known as the Suffragette Arboretum. Between 1909 and 1911, at least 47 trees were planted in the grounds of Eagle House, with different species of trees marking different aspects of the Suffragette movement. Holly trees, for example, were planted for those involved in the movement in general and conifers for a woman who had been imprisoned. All of the trees in the arboretum apart from the Austrian pine planted by Rose Lamartine Yates were sadly destroyed in the late 1960s to make way for a housing estate.

Unveiling a memorial to the Suffragette movement in 2024, vice-chair of Bath & North East Somerset Council, Liz Hardman, described Batheaston as once harbouring a 'nest of Suffragettes' thanks to the 'forward-thinking' Blathwayts. Visitors to Eagle House, who included Emmeline Pankhurst, used its summerhouse for welcome rest and recuperation after speaking tours or spells in prison. The memorial is contained within a decommissioned telephone box that Batheaston Parish Council bought for just £1. Its location is apt as it is positioned on the boundary of the original walled garden to Eagle House and its former arboretum. 'The phone box will now tell this extraordinary, factual story of a life long gone,' says Hardman. 'And yet one most cherished by women who simply just wanted to have the same privilege as men – to be able to cast their vote.'

ADDRESS Corner of Eagle Road and Northend, BA1 7HS TIP Two trees in Royal Victoria Park and Alice Park have been planted to commemorate the lost arboretum following a campaign led by a group of history lecturers and researchers at Bath Spa University.

91 Sycamore Gap Sapling

Keeping joy and hope alive

When the Sycamore Gap tree at Hadrian's Wall in Northumberland was illegally felled in 2023, there was sadness across the globe. Like Bath, Hadrian's Wall is a World Heritage Site and the much-loved tree had been a landmark for almost 200 years.

While the original tree cannot be directly replaced, 49 'Trees of Hope' Sycamore Gap saplings have been gifted by the National Trust to sites across the UK. The number of saplings is significant as it represents each foot in height that the tree was at the time of its felling. Out of nearly 500 applications for the saplings, one group from Bath was successful. All the saplings have been planted in publicly accessible locations, including the Alder Hey Children's Hospital in Liverpool, Battersea Park in London and the Balfour Memorial Garden in Orkney, as well as all 15 UK National Parks.

Sycamore 'is one of the most architecturally beautiful trees in our landscape', says independent Trees of Hope judge and arboriculture specialist Catherine Nuttgens. 'In summer, their dark green leaves create a canopy that looks almost like broccoli. While in winter, they create a silhouette that perfectly depicts what we think of when we think of a tree. The loss of any tree can evoke strong emotions; none more so than the Sycamore Gap tree. Its destruction felt utterly senseless, destroying the simple joy it brought to so many people for so many reasons. But the Trees of Hope initiative has kept that sense of joy and hope alive. And it has been truly humbling to read through so many applications.'

Bath's Sycamore Gap sapling was planted in Alice Park in February 2026 thanks to a successful application from the Alice Park Trust. The sapling is dedicated to children and young people living in care or care-experienced, with members of the mental health and wellbeing charity Off the Record helping to organise the planting.

ADDRESS Alice Park, Gloucester Road, BA1 7BL, www.nationaltrust.org.uk/treesofhope **TIP** Alice Park Café was originally the changing room for cricket and football teams at Alice Park (www.alicepark.co.uk/cafe).

92 Temperance Hall

From escaping alcohol to an escape room

A blog by Andrew Davison on the Historic England website in 2026 calls temperance 'one of the most influential movements in 19th-century England'. Temperance Hall in Bath, squeezed onto a narrow site in Widcombe, dates from 1847, just over a decade since the first temperance societies were established as a consequence of poverty and social distress caused by alcohol abuse. Now used for a widely different purpose, this 'handsome little building' according to Pevsner's *Architectural Guide to Bath* shows just how much society has changed in more than 175 years.

According to Davison, temperance reformers created an 'entire parallel infrastructure' of buildings and institutions due to their exclusion from alcohol-focused public spaces. At the start of the temperance movement in the 1830s, there were few public halls, with meetings held at inns whose main purpose was selling alcohol. Being unwilling to hold their own meetings in these dens of iniquity, reformers raised money to buy or build their own premises, and by 1853, more than 300 temperance halls existed across England – from simple wooden huts to grand buildings. Within them, meetings and lectures took place, as well as dances and theatrical performances. There were also hundreds of temperance hotels nationwide, alcohol-free coffee taverns and billiard halls, and water fountains.

After the demise of the temperance movement, the hall was later used by the International Order of Good Templars and the Independent Order of Rechabites, and then became the Church of the Nazarene and later the place of worship for the First Church of Christ, Scientist. The Grade II-listed building is now home to escape room Tempo Bath, with recent games based around themes including *Raiders of the Lost Ark* and finding the key to eternal life – the latter perhaps helped by never drinking a drop of alcohol.

ADDRESS Tempo Bath, Claverton Street, BA2 4LE, +44 (0)1225 962994, www.tempo-bath.com **TIP** St Mark's Community Centre in the former St Mark's Church near Temperance Hall hosts a variety of events, including fitness classes, barn dances and live music (www.stmarkscc.co.uk).

93 Temple Ornament

All that remains of a former chapel

The railway is to blame for this unusual structure close to one corner of Queen Square. In the shadow of an evergreen tree, it might appear out of place until you learn its history. Because this was originally the location of St Mary's Chapel, opened on Christmas Day 1734 to serve the residents of the newly constructed Queen Square. The chapel was Bath's earliest proprietary chapel – built by subscription and maintained by private individuals. This one was built for the sum of £2,000 for a consortium of architect John Wood and 11 other residents. Why schlep into town from your new home if you could build your own place of worship on your doorstep? *Pevsner's Architectural Guide* calls the former chapel a 'fine classical temple'. It was set back and accessible from Chapel Row, with the name of this small road a clue as to what was once here.

The chapel was demolished in 1875 for road widening in order to improve access to Green Park station. Temple Ornament was created a few years after the demise of the chapel using fragments from its once grand structure. The artist is unknown. A column from the chapel can also be seen in the garden at 4 Cleveland Place near Cleveland Bridge. A plaque on the base of the Temple Ornament says it was *re-erected in 1976 after its restoration by students of Bath Technical College*. Another plaque nearby marks the site of the chapel, informing us that was *erected for subscribers residing in this area and sited to close the western vista across the south side of the square.*

While St Mary's Chapel was demolished, the Victorian French Gothic edifice of the former Holy Trinity Church, also with one side facing Chapel Row, has recently been transformed into a co-working space by Gather Round (www.gather-round.co/locations/trinity-church). Flooded with natural light, the building also contains private studios and event spaces.

ADDRESS Chapel Row, BA1 2HN TIP Opposite the Temple Ornament is Corkage, an award-winning independent restaurant with one of Bath's best wine lists (www.corkagebath.com).

94 Theatre of the Railway

Brunel's only surviving cast-iron bridge

Opened in 1795, Sydney Gardens was originally laid out as the largest pleasure gardens outside London, containing a multitude of entertainments. There were orchestras playing, a grotto with a hermit puppet, a waterfall and a labyrinth. Just five years after the gardens opened, the Kennet & Avon Canal was dug through them, skilfully adding to its beauty. But when the arrival of the railway in 1840 threatened to cut the park in two, the gardens were already past their prime and the city fathers agreed that compensation money would more than make up for the loss of attractions including the labyrinth.

The chief railway engineer, Isambard Kingdom Brunel, still had the responsibility of not destroying the unique character of the park despite slicing it in half. He oversaw the planting of trees and lawns, and designed both stone and cast-iron footbridges over the railway line, which have been popular places for train enthusiasts ever since. Brunel even considered erecting a single-storey pavilion for an even better vantage point but this idea never left the drawing board.

In 2025, Network Rail submitted a planning application to Bath & North East Somerset Council so repairs can be allowed to take place to the remaining cast-iron footbridge. Currently in poor condition, it is the only survivor of many designed by Brunel along the GWR line between London and Bristol. According to Network Rail's planning application, 'Brunel's railway intervention altered Sydney Gardens substantially from its earlier Georgian state. Brunel's theatrical engineering, however, provided a new leisure attraction for the age – trainspotting – and has been physically entwined with what is today a key asset of the World Heritage Site ever since'. The restoration of the footbridge hopes to preserve the 'Brunelian' experience and this 'theatre of the railway'.

ADDRESS Sydney Gardens, Sydney Place, Bathwick, BA2 6NH, www.bathnes.gov.uk/visit-sydney-gardens TIP The Holburne Museum in Sydney Gardens was Bath's first public art gallery. In 2024, Mr Doodle filled its walls, floors and ceilings with his doodles (www.holburne.org).

95 Titanic's Oldest Survivor

The 'unsinkable' Edwina Troutt

Former Bath mayor Bryan Chalker is to thank for a plaque commemorating Edwina Troutt. Bath-born Edwina, better known as Winnie, died in 1984 at the age of 100, and the plaque says she was *Titanic*'s oldest survivor. It was a fact she believed to be true until her death in California. But another woman, Mary Davis, actually held the longevity record for *Titanic* survivors, according to the *Encyclopedia Titanica*. Mary, who died in 1987 aged 104, was born in London on 18 May 1883, making her just over a year older than Winnie, who was born in Bath on 8 July 1884.

Regardless of the actual accolade, Winnie had an extraordinary life. One of more than 10 children, her family lived at 40 Claverton Street and 13 Newark Street. After emigrating to the USA, she worked as a domestic servant, including a spell for Harry Garfield, whose father James had been assassinated while serving as US president. She found her way onto a lifeboat lowered from the *Titanic* after being handed a baby whose mother had already left the ship. Later in life, she picked apricots for use in the manufacture of gas masks and her first husband was a former baker to the Danish royal family.

Bath's connection to the *Titanic* does not end here. Winnie's fellow Bathonian, Edwin 'Fred' Wheeler, was another passenger on board the ill-fated ship but he did not survive and was one of some 1,500 people who perished in the icy waters of the North Atlantic Ocean on 15 April 1912. Edwin was 26 when he died, having been on board the *Titanic* as a second-class passenger. His main purpose during the voyage was to chaperone the luggage of his employers, the Vanderbilts, one of the wealthiest families in the USA.

Edwina and Edwin might also have seen some electric deck-cranes on the *Titanic* that had been manufactured in Bath by Stothert & Pitt, with the firm also making boiler parts for the liner.

ADDRESS Newark Street, BA1 1AP TIP Phone boxes within SouthGate shopping centre are filled with flowers all year round.

96 Toad Patrol

How did the toads cross the road?

A road sign on Charlcombe Lane is unlike any you have probably seen. It features the silhouette of a toad because this is one of only four places in the UK where a road is closed to allow them to cross. Not just toads either but also frogs and newts, with the slippery trio crossing in their thousands every year to reach their ancestral breeding lake in the valley below.

A half-mile (800-metre) stretch of road has been closed for six weeks since 2003, with volunteers from the Charlcombe Toad Rescue Group going out on patrol each night during this period from early February to help the creatures on their journey. With the road free of motor vehicles, dozens of volunteers pick up the toads, frogs and newts using latex gloves to avoid contamination, and safely transport them to drop-off points near the breeding lake. Some 50,000 creatures have been helped to cross the road this way since 2003.

This may be one of only four roads closed for the annual migration but there are more than 200 other toad patrols across the UK who help amphibians deal with one of their biggest challenges: road traffic. Another challenge for the tiny critters is the loss of habitat, with data collected by national toad patrols showing the common toad population has declined by 41 per cent in 40 years. Amphibians help maintain ecosystems, with toads and frogs predators to insects and prey for bigger animals. Frogs' susceptibility to pollution means they can also signal problems with an environment.

Charlcombe Toad Rescue Group manager Helen Hobbs says the closure helps the population of amphibians in Bath buck national trends and stand 'a fighting chance of flourishing'. In 2026, Helen told BBC News: 'With a changing climate it is becoming increasingly difficult to predict the peak times for amphibian movements. That is why closing the road for six weeks makes such a difference.'

ADDRESS Charlcombe Lane, BA1 8DS (what3words: puts.level.glad)
TIP Jane Austen was a fan of this corner of Bath. A slate within a wall near the road sign is a diary entry of hers from 2 June 1799: *We took a charming walk to Charlcombe sweetly situated in a little green valley.*

97 Topping & Co Ladders

Where fiction meets reality

You need to walk up some stairs to get to books about fashion and photography. You need to walk down some stairs to get to books about science and sport. And if want to reach books on any number of subjects that have been placed on the top shelves of Toppings, you need to climb up some ladders. It seems a missed opportunity to put mountain literature (A–Z by author) on the easily accessible lower shelves. In the shop's biography section, Walt Disney and John F. Kennedy are at the top, and Kelly Holmes and Madonna towards the bottom. A biography of the Brontë sisters is on the bottom shelf, while some of their works are up a ladder in the nearby fiction section.

'Please use with care. Do ask if you would like some help,' says a sign on each ladder, many of which curve around corners and slide in a splendidly satisfying way. The ladders are within the great hall and the lower hall at Toppings, a quite brilliant bookshop spread across three floors that has a map outside to enable visitors to find their way around. One ladder near a grandfather clock is next to the only books you are unable to browse as they are kept behind glass screens under lock and key. Most of the hardback tomes in here are signed first editions, including *Normal People* by Sally Rooney (£615) and *Life* by Keith Richards (£1,000).

Topping & Co's premises on York Street, which they moved into in 2021, was built as a Masonic lodge, and later became an assembly rooms and Quaker meeting house. Celebrity chef Raymond Blanc had wanted to turn it into a restaurant but that came to nothing and Bath-based architect Mark Wray, whose dream job was to design a shop, was appointed by Robert Topping to open a much larger store, having outgrown his previous premises on the Paragon. Writing in the *Royal Institute of British Architects Journal*, Eleanor Young called Wray's commission a 'fantasy-project-come true'.

ADDRESS York Street, BA1 1NG, +44 (0)1225 428111, www.toppingbooks.co.uk
TIP Bayntun-Riviere within George Bayntun on Manvers Street is a bookbinder dating back to 1829 that claims to have the largest collection of hand tools and blocks in the world (www.georgebayntun.com).

98 Tucking Mill Viaduct

View into Bath's rich Victorian railway heritage

If you ever happen to find yourself in the Spanish city of Segovia, you will soon notice that locals like to meet 'debajo del acueducto' – underneath the aqueduct. Still standing since being constructed by the Romans in around AD 50, its 167 arches carried water to the city from nearby mountains using just gravity. The Romans in Bath did not have to overcome similar challenges to transport water into Aquae Sulis but their Victorian successors built a viaduct for different purposes, with its construction sharing many of the techniques used by their Roman forebears.

Five arches form Tucking Mill Viaduct – considerably less than its Segovian counterpart but no less impressive as an insight into Bath's rich Victorian railway heritage. The viaduct was built in the 1870s on the route of the former Somerset & Dorset Railway as it made its way through the picturesque Midford Valley. It now forms part of the Two Tunnels Greenway and a runner with their head down or cyclist looking to achieve a Strava segment personal best could easily miss the fact that they are travelling over the impressive span. Pause for a picnic on a handily located bench next to the viaduct to take in your stunning surroundings.

The best view of the viaduct is down a footpath close to the southern portal of the Combe Down Tunnel, which takes you next to Tucking Mill Reservoir. The reservoir is now owned by Wessex Water and designed especially for visitors with disabilities to enjoy angling free of charge. Wheelchair-accessible platforms are large enough for two wheelchairs, with the lake stocked with plenty of fish.

Tucking Mill is named after a mill building that once stood close to the entrance gates to the site, with the remains of the mill demolished in 1979 to make way for the present lake over which the viaduct was built to carry the railway on its way to Bath.

ADDRESS Tucking Mill, BA2 7DB **TIP** Bath asparagus, also known as Spiked Star of Bethlehem, is among the plants and wildflowers that grow in the woodlands around Tucking Mill.

99 Twerton Park

Terraces not armchairs

The floodlights at Twerton Park acted like a beacon on a recent Tuesday night. This stadium has been Bath City's ground since 1932 and in that time, it has also been the temporary home of Bristol Rovers from 1986 to 1996 and Bristol City Women in the 2020–21 season when global superstar, former US captain and twice World Cup winner Alex Morgan, played under Twerton's floodlights.

In 2026, there was a campaign to keep these floodlights turned on, with £100,000 needing to be raised to upgrade the lights so football can continue to be played at Twerton Park. 'This campaign is about more than funding,' says the club website. 'It's about showing what this club means to the city and what this community can achieve together.' Before a match in the National League South against Slough Town, volunteers in the ticket office and shop were guessing the attendance to be from 700 to 950 (it was 744 fans who eventually watched a 1-0 defeat – some way from Twerton's record attendance of 18,020 in 1960) and one fan asked for a shout-out to Paul Hill who was celebrating his 48th birthday.

'Aquae Sulis, terraces not armchairs,' says one flag on display at Twerton Park. Is this a sly dig at their egg-chasing neighbours? In the grandstand here, the bobbing and weaving of fans' heads is like a boxer in the ring because of half a dozen or so pillars holding up the corrugated iron roof. Before kick-off, queues formed outside the MoBQue. Warm your cockles as generations of football fans have done before you with a cup of Bovril. 'Ready to Go' by Republica, 'The Final Countdown' by Europe and 'Right Here, Right Now' by Fatboy Slim played as kick-off neared, with unofficial club anthem 'Go Bath City Go' by Hacksaw being the final song before the referee blew his whistle for the match to start. 'Get behind the City and enjoy the game!' shouted the announcer over the tannoy.

ADDRESS High Street, BA2 1DB, +44 (0)1225 423087, www.bathcityfc.com
TIP A mural of Bath City's most famous fan, film director Ken Loach, by street artist Stewy, is on the side of 117 High Street, a stone's throw from the ground (www.stewy.uk).

100 Two Tunnels Greenway

The UK's longest walking and cycling tunnel

Cycling through one of the two tunnels that make up the Two Tunnels Greenway becomes almost hypnotic. Pick a hot summer's day to traverse the tunnels and feel the cool air of the shafts even before you enter them. Once you are inside, you just keep going like Dory in *Finding Nemo*, the lights on either side guiding your subterranean journey between Bath and Midford.

Two Tunnels Greenway, an extension of Linear Park, is a four-mile section of what used to be the Somerset & Dorset Railway between Bath and Bournemouth. Once carrying holidaymakers, commuters and coal from the Somerset coalfields, Linear Park was created as Bath's first 'natural' park, aiming to create the feel of a country lane surrounded by trees, shrubs and flowers common to the English countryside.

The northern portal of the Devonshire Tunnel had been buried beneath tonnes of earth following the railway's closure; and it was not until 2013 that the Devonshire and Combe Down tunnels, as well as the nearby Tucking Mill Viaduct, were reopened following a successful restoration that saw the trackbed becoming a traffic-free walking and cycling route as part of the National Cycle Network. At just over a mile long (1.6 kilometres), the Combe Down Tunnel – which steam trains first used in 1874 as the longest railway tunnel in the UK without ventilation shafts – is now the country's longest walking and cycling tunnel, having been the longest in Europe when it opened.

When the Combe Down Tunnel and its cutting were first excavated, it revealed four different layers of rock dating back about 170 million years to the Jurassic period. Land surveyor William Smith recorded these rocks and showed how they could be identified by the fossils they contain. Geological maps made by Smith, known as 'the father of English geology', were among the first to be published anywhere in the world.

ADDRESS Between Bath and Midford, www.twotunnels.org.uk TIP Look out for three sculptures close to the entrance of the Devonshire Tunnel. Chosen by pupils from Oldfield Park Junior School, they are Winter Olympics gold medallist Amy Williams, the 'last fighting Tommy' Harry Patch, and a Roman centurion.

101 The Undefended City

When Bath was targeted for being beautiful

Scars that can clearly still be seen on the side of one city centre building are a visible reminder of the devastation wrought on Bath during World War II. Nisbets is the former Labour Exchange where the council helped those looking for work and paid out subsistence money. After being badly damaged in two bombing raids, it continued to function within the stump of its former self.

The bombardment of Bath by the German Luftwaffe between 25 and 27 April 1942 was part of what has become known as the 'Baedeker raids' – the targeting of sites of historic importance that did not have gun defences, named after German travel guides and in response to RAF raids on German civilian targets. Some 240 bombs were dropped on Bath, resulting in the deaths of 417 people and injury to around 1,000. Many residents ignored the first warning sirens since they assumed that the planes would be targeting Bristol as they had done for the previous few months. The Labour Exchange was just one of 19,000 buildings that were damaged.

Oldfield Park was one Bath neighbourhood that was hit hard by the Luftwaffe. A public air raid shelter on Moorland Road took a direct hit, resulting in numerous deaths. On the site of the shelter now stands a small park and memorial garden where, in 2008, former bomber pilot Willi Schludecker took part in a service and apologised for his part in the raids. Within the memorial garden is a plaque remembering the 63 children who were killed in the raids, including all seven Rattray children between 10 months and 13 years old, and six Ford children killed in New King Street.

'The war between our two countries caused dreadful damage to towns and cities on both sides, and the citizens of both of our countries paid a heavy price,' says Willi on his visit to Bath. 'War is madness. Let us together think of and honour all of those victims in a credible way.'

ADDRESS Nisbets, 1–3 James Street West, BA1 2BX TIP The Bath Blitz Memorial Project is an online resource showing the locations of all bomb locations across the city, as well as preserving personal memories (www.bathheritagewatchdog.org/bathblitz).

102 The Urban Garden

Green-fingered goodness

Within part of the council-run nursery, The Urban Garden is a treasure trove. They call themselves 'the smallest garden centre with the biggest heart' and have a multitude of items for sale from pots to pond plants, seeds to shrubs, but also help young unemployed people back into work. So buying a plant or a pot here, a coffee or tea from a converted horse-box on-site, or giving a donation at the till, means you are providing vital funds to support The Urban Garden's horticultural therapy and training programme for adults who are unemployed or struggling with their mental health. It's their main aim and the reason why The Urban Garden was created: to help people with life challenges improve their wellbeing, and move further towards work and education.

The numbers speak for themselves. Each year since The Urban Garden opened in 2021, it has supported 28 people to achieve either a level 1 or 2 City & Guilds qualification in practical horticulture, supported 12 trainees on their work experience programme and helped more than 10 people into employment.

Just months after The Urban Garden opened, the crucial work they do was praised by Bath's MP, Wera Hobhouse. 'It was lovely to visit The Urban Garden who do so much for the community,' Hobhouse says. 'The site offers the perfect combination of sustainable practices and training for young unemployed people to get back into work. I couldn't resist buying some of the plants and I would encourage anyone to head down if they are into gardening.'

Committed and skilled volunteers are always needed to help in the garden centre. Or if you're just coming to shop, The Urban Garden is the sort of place it's almost impossible to leave empty-handed. Even if you don't have a garden at home, you won't feel left out thanks to items including make-your-own terrarium kits, new and second-hand books, honey and soaps.

ADDRESS Marlborough Buildings, BA1 2LZ, +44 (0)877 846488, www.theurbangarden.org.uk TIP The Botanical Gardens in Royal Victoria Park are free to enter. They contain botanical plants and flowers as well as a replica Roman temple (www.bathnes.gov.uk/botanical-gardens).

103 Victoria Bridge

A full-scale advertisement

Any suspension bridge in the South West of England undoubtedly lies in the shadow of the Clifton Suspension Bridge in Bristol. If things had gone differently, however, the designer of that span might not have been Isambard Kingdom Brunel but James Dredge. One footbridge by Dredge still stands in Bath, where it acted as a full-scale advertisement for his engineering prowess. Opened in 1836, it was Dredge's first attempt at a novel method of construction at a time when steel had yet to be invented. Battling against the expense of wrought iron, Dredge invented a taper chain that progressively used less iron towards the bridge's centre.

Dredge did not begin his career as an engineer but as a brewer, with Victoria Bridge acting as a link to transport his beer across the River Avon from the Lower Bristol Road to the Upper Bristol Road. The business-minded Dredge marketed Victoria Bridge as a demonstration model of his design, which despite appearances is not a suspension bridge but a hybrid between a suspension and a cable-stayed bridge. In the words of Bath Heritage Watchdog, it has 'two opposing cantilevers which meet in the middle of the span, and the use of inclined hangers introduces an element of compression into the road-bearing deck which stabilises the structure from strong side-winds'.

Years of neglect led to the bridge being closed due to safety issues in 2010 but work got underway in 2014 on a £3.4 million refurbishment project. Victorian engineers would not have been too enamoured with their modern-day successors, however, with defects identified in the structure's new surface just weeks after the bridge had been reopened in 2015. A few sections of the anti-slip surface had come away from some of the timber decking planks, with contractors needing to refit the surfacing using a different method. Not the best advertisement for their prowess.

ADDRESS Victoria Bridge Road, BA1 3AY **TIP** Bijou Bikeworks on Victoria Bridge Road is both a bike shop and a café (www.bijoubikeworks.com).

104 Wansdyke

A mysterious link with the past

Maybe you are reading this on a Wednesday. If so, then it is 'Woden's Day' – named after the supreme Saxon pagan god. Woden also happened to be the god of tribal boundaries, which is apt for the Wansdyke whose name has evolved over the centuries from its original Anglo Saxon moniker of 'Woden's Ditch'.

The Wansdyke is an ancient linear earthwork comprising a bank with a ditch on one side. It is among the longest earthworks of its period in England; around 50 miles (80 kilometres) long and up to 100 feet (30 metres) wide, with the ditch 4 to 5 metres wide and 2 to 3 metres deep. The 2 to 3 metre-high bank was made mainly of material excavated from the ditch and originally topped with turf, timber or stones. Its precise route around Bath is uncertain but experts believe it runs north of Horsecombe Vale, south of Prior Park and may form part of the earthworks on Bathampton Down.

One of the most intriguing elements about this mysterious link with the past is that a lack of archaeological and historical evidence means much of the information about the Wansdyke is just guesswork. Theories include that its construction was to create a boundary in the 5th century between native British territories. Or it could have been built by the native Britons to keep out Anglo Saxon invaders. Or it might have been built in the 7th century by the West Saxons. The likeliest theory is that it was built in the late or early post-Roman period during the 5th century.

Whoever built it, its purpose was certainly to define a boundary and is evidence of some major former divisions across what is now England, forming an important frontier built by those to the south in order to control access to their land. And its function as a boundary continues to this day with the Wansdyke east of the Sulis Meadows housing estate remaining as a parish boundary after more than 1,000 years.

ADDRESS Wansdyke Path, BA2 5RY TIP Castle Farm in Midford is a restaurant in a barn on an organic farm with a variety of different dining experiences (www.castlefarmmidford.co.uk).

105 Warleigh Weir Sauna

Reconnecting with nature

While you are sitting inside Aether Sauna, a view of the natural world opens up in front of you, predominantly of water but also plenty of greenery. The cedar-lined sauna is located at Warleigh Weir, which has long been a popular outdoor swimming spot. This new addition on the land creates an extra element to proceedings and is also going some way in helping to establish a British sauna culture, with the South West experiencing a rapid growth in saunas over recent years.

Other saunas have ice baths or cold plunge pools – varying temperatures just as it was done in Roman times – but Aether Sauna has the River Avon just a few steps away if the heat gets too intense and you want cooling down. Enjoy a cold river dip and then get back into the sauna. The main line to Weymouth is also nearby but the occasional sound of trains just adds to the atmosphere.

Aether Sauna is partly inspired by the social aspects of Turkish community saunas and the nature connection from indigenous 'sweat lodge' ceremonies, but it also aims to become a new version of the British pub with its humour and sense of community. Guests are encouraged to get to know each other by talking as the session progresses. Sessions are all introduced by your resident 'Gusmeister' because Aether Sauna specialises in 'Aufguss', a version of guided sauna. At each session, the Gusmeister will introduce scents (perhaps from rosemary, lavender and sage grown on the land here) into the sauna, play music, and maybe share some ideas and thoughts.

Warleigh Weir and sauna owner, Johnny Palmer, has become an experienced Gusmeister and may well be taking the 90-minute session you book. Aether Sauna is a combination of Johnny's newfound adoption of Aufguss combined with his love of wild swimming, as well as his skills in connecting people, which here is done in the heat overlooking the natural world.

ADDRESS Ferry Lane, Claverton, BA2 7BH, +44 (0)7748 102844, www.aethersauna.co.uk TIP If you don't want a sauna session, just enjoy hanging out at Warleigh Weir (www.warleighweir.co.uk).

106 Watchman's Sentry Box

What's going on in here then?

Before the creation of police forces in England and Wales in the middle of the 19th century, it was parishes who employed watchmen to patrol the streets at night, deterring criminality and hopefully providing a reassuring presence. Despite their important job, these men were widely disliked and regularly lampooned in caricatures. The system was also known for corruption, incompetence and drunkenness, often attracting elderly men or former soldiers.

If you wanted to find a watchman, there would be no better way than looking for a watchman's sentry box. On the corner of the triangular green in front of Norfolk Crescent (named after Nelson's home county), there is a box from around 1810 thought to have been designed by John Palmer, also believed to have been the architect of the crescent. So, the cylindrical sentry box made from Bath stone was originally created to blend in seamlessly with its surroundings. This one is described by English Heritage as 'a very rare survivor of this building type, revealing a high level of architectural finish'. Its look may have been influenced by the Choragic Monument of Lysicrates near the Acropolis in Athens, popular to emulate in Georgian Britain.

The gates to the Holburne Museum are flanked by a pair of watchman's boxes dating back to 1830. These would originally have been built into the boundary wall of a former hotel and likely never had doors, making their function perhaps more ornamental than practical.

The job of watchmen included calling out the time and announcing the weather. They would usually work in pairs, with a box such as this one on Norfolk Crescent providing them with shelter before the end of their shift at 7am in winter and 5am during the rest of the year. If a watchman apprehended a miscreant, he would have been kept overnight within a larger watch-house, before being marched to a magistrate in the morning.

ADDRESS Norfolk Crescent Open Space, BA1 2TL TIP Close to another corner of the green in front of Norfolk Crescent is BRaC, a speciality coffee and focaccia sandwich shop (www.instagram.com/brac____).

107 Widcombe Lock Flight

With the second deepest lock in the UK

Nobody wants 'extensive puddling' following heavy rain. But that's one of the weaknesses identified in the character of Widcombe in an appraisal of the conservation area by Bath & North East Somerset Council in 2020. More specifically, the puddles are on the canal towpath towards Bathwick, which was said to be 'in a poor state of repair'. The Kennet & Avon Canal and neighbouring riverside are praised, however, as providing 'a green corridor and the opportunity for wildlife, trees and other plants to thrive side by side with the city centre, as well as an important setting for the buildings nearby'.

Before the arrival of the canal, which was completed in 1810, Widcombe was a desirable residential area thanks to its position on the verdant slopes high above the smoky city. It is viewed by its residents today as 'the place where the city meets the countryside'. The area's topography explains why Widcombe Lock Flight contains the second deepest lock in the UK, with locks 8 and 9 combined in the 1970s due to road reconstruction into a single 19-foot-high (6-metre-high) lock. Between the top of the flight and the River Avon is a 65-foot (20 metre) vertical drop and six locks through which to navigate. Every boat passing through the flight uses an entire lockful of water – equivalent to about 1,000 bathtubs. The Kennet & Avon Canal runs for 87 miles (140 kilometres) and links the Bristol Channel with London. It never really flourished as an industrial waterway with the Great Western Railway making it virtually redundant.

Like locks? In total, the Canal & River Trust maintains and protects 1,589 of them. The longest lock flight in the UK is the Tardebigge Flight on the Worcester & Birmingham Canal that boasts 30 locks and raises the canal 220 feet (67 metres). Beating Bath into second place for the UK's deepest lock is Tuel Lane Lock on the Rochdale Canal that measures almost 20 feet (6 metres) from top to bottom.

ADDRESS Next to St Matthew's Place, BA2 4JJ TIP Widcombe Social Club on Widcombe Hill hosts live music, films and classes, with music and pizza nights every Friday (www.widcombesocialclub.co.uk).

108 Wild Walcot

Tackling the ecological emergency head-on

Next to Bath's former corn market – which a wry joke goes has had scaffolding on one side of it for so long that the poles and planks themselves are listed – is a small garden on what was once wasteland, hemmed in by wooden fence panels whose blue paint is now chipping off. A bench is a sunny place to sit as cars come and go from the nearby Cattle Market Car Park, whose livestock are long gone but where an antique and flea market takes place every Saturday.

The garden is the most visible part of Wild Walcot, a community partnership that hoped to establish 'a wildlife-friendly green corridor' along the length of Walcot Street. Planters along the road containing a variety of greenery were sponsored by local businesses and anyone could volunteer in the garden. Volunteers learned new skills and knowledge about plants and wildlife-friendly gardening with this oasis still providing a rich source of food for pollinators, and shelter for invertebrates and birds. A note in the garden contains photos of several species and a few words on how to look after them. Salad burnet and wild clary, for example, are both accustomed to taking care of themselves, but honeysuckle might need the occasional prune.

From a small window in the Honey Café within the vaults of St Swithin's Church – one of the sponsors of a Wild Walcot planter – is an elevated vantage point of Walcot Street, winding down the hill with the spire of St Michael's Church in the distance. Close to the church is a shopfront with the hand-painted sign of *Slowly Downward*. This is in fact the gallery space of Stanley Donwood (www.slowlydownward.com), an artist best known for his work with Radiohead. If you are a fan of the band, look out for familiar artwork in the window, including the creature with pointy teeth known as the Radiohead bear, and one of the Oxford band's most well-known visual identities.

ADDRESS Garden is next to 62 Walcot Street, BA1 5BD TIP For most of the 1970s, 146 Walcot Street was the headquarters of Bath Arts Workshop, whose anarchic activities were covered by Terry Pratchett during his time as a local journalist.

109 William Wilberforce Plaque

Remembering a frequent visitor to Bath

William Wilberforce is remembered on a plaque in Great Pulteney Street close to the Holburne Museum. But the anti-slavery campaigner was a regular visitor to Bath and a plaque could have been erected in any number of places. He was married to Barbara Spooner at St Swithin's Church in 1797. Barbara's parents lived in the Royal Crescent, where he stayed in the winter of 1798, and he also stayed at 9 North Parade in 1831.

Wilberforce was a politician and philanthropist best known for his role in the struggle to abolish the slave trade and then to abolish slavery itself. He was plagued by ill health for most of his adult life, developing ulcerative colitis in his 20s and a curvature of the spine in his 50s. And so, where better to visit than Bath? He married Barbara within just six weeks of meeting her and the couple continued to visit regularly, even buying an estate at West Wick between Bath and Bristol. In 1821, they were in Bath with their eldest daughter, also called Barbara, who was taking the waters in an attempt to cure her tuberculosis.

Many famous people have plaques to their memory in Bath. These include Wilberforce's friend, former prime minister William Pitt the Younger (15 Johnstone Street); poet William Wordsworth (9 North Parade); admiral Horatio Nelson (2 Pierrepont Street); explorer David Livingstone (13 The Circus); and novelist Charles Dickens (35 St James' Square). Men unfortunately vastly outnumber women. But look out for a plaque commemorating Bath's most famous former resident, Jane Austen, at 4 Sydney Place. Elsewhere, find archaeological artist and explorer Adela Breton at 15 Camden Crescent; author Sarah Fielding at Widcombe Lodge on Widcombe Hill; and musician Elizabeth Linley at Linley House on Pierrepont Place.

ADDRESS 36 Great Pulteney Street, BA2 4BZ TIP On the corner of Great Pulteney Street and Edward Street is a rare surviving example of a Queen Victoria Penfold post box, a hexagonal pillar box designed by J. W. Penfold in 1866 with a decorative acanthus leaf cap.

110 Worldbuilders of Queen Street

Get lost within different worlds

Nothing beats a good explore and nothing is quite like the Worldbuilders of Queen Street. The journey you take is up to you but the recommended route is to start in the basement and then work up each of the building's five storeys. It's one of those places best discovered yourself with instructions to open drawers, handle objects and 'interact freely with the space'. What this means is completely up to you but there will always be three different worlds to explore based around science fiction and fantasy, with the rooms a real-life extension of the books that the Worldbuilders of Queen Street also publish.

You might even find artist Oliver Hurst in his studio on the second floor of this 1760s Georgian townhouse. Many of Oliver's original oil paintings are dotted around the building and are available to buy if you want to take a bit of a particular world home with you. Follow your nose to his studio and watch a different reality come to life through the medium of oil. Oliver is part of sci-fi authorship trio K. M. Moke alongside creator Mark Warrick and writer Kelly Townley; their first novel based in the world of Evol was published in 2026. As the world developed, so did the concept art and early drafts, with the first quarter of what would become *The Evol Algorithm* available to buy here before the end of the book had even been completed.

Evol creator Mark is also the principal creator of the worlds on exhibition at the Worldbuilders. He has explained that J. R. R. Tolkien was a worldbuilder and a linguist long before being a storyteller. 'People never really spoke about his worldbuilding; they spoke about the story. Worldbuilding has since become a skill, a craft and a real creative endeavour. So we want to represent that as a building and as an experience.'

ADDRESS 12 Queen Street, BA1 1HE, www.worldbuildersofqueenstreet.com
TIP Worldbuilders of Queen Street work collaboratively with Mr B's Emporium of Reading Delights, a superb bookshop only a few hundred yards away on John Street which celebrated its 20th birthday in 2026 (www.mrbsemporium.com).

111 The Yellow Shop

A riot of colour among Bath's beige

It's impossible to miss The Yellow Shop. If it's not its colour that first attracts you, it might be the flag. Or it could be the sign similar to the Chupa Chups logo. Or it could be the waving cats or Playmobil figures in the window, the glitter ball or the sound of music from within. You might even be a Van Morrison fan, paying homage to the front cover of his 2002 album 'Down the Road', which features this shopfront.

The Yellow Shop sells retro and vintage clothing but is so much more. This is a place of connection; holding a flame to a Bath of not so long ago that has now all but disappeared. On a recent morning, two friends who had not seen each other for years caught up for a chat on one of the benches outside. After they walked away, shop owner Clare De-Pulford had to run after them as one of the women had left her coat behind.

Soaking up the sun on the now empty bench, Clare explained that when she moved to Bath at 16, the city was very different: 'There was a real counter-culture and Walcot Street was central to that.' Clare worked for the previous owner for 15 years before she became the custodian of The Yellow Shop, which has always been a yellow shop, hence the name. 'We've lost our venues, we've lost our local places, we've lost our local people, Bath has become gentrified.' So to counter this, Clare's shop is a place for community, regularly inviting anyone who wants to DJ on the shop floor to drop in. 'We open up the doors, we try to encourage that kind of vibe, just a place for people to meet.'

Located right above The Yellow Shop is American Dream Comics (www.americandreamcomics.co.uk), another shop like nothing else in Bath. Clare's collectibles and toys downstairs might not be for sale but they most definitely are here alongside comic books, graphic novels, trading cards and assorted merchandise for all of your favourite fictional characters.

ADDRESS 72 Walcot Street, BA1 5BD, +44 (0)1225 404001, www.theyellowshopbath.co.uk TIP The Bell on Walcot Street is a community-owned pub with a bohemian spirit and regular live music (www.thebellinnbath.co.uk).

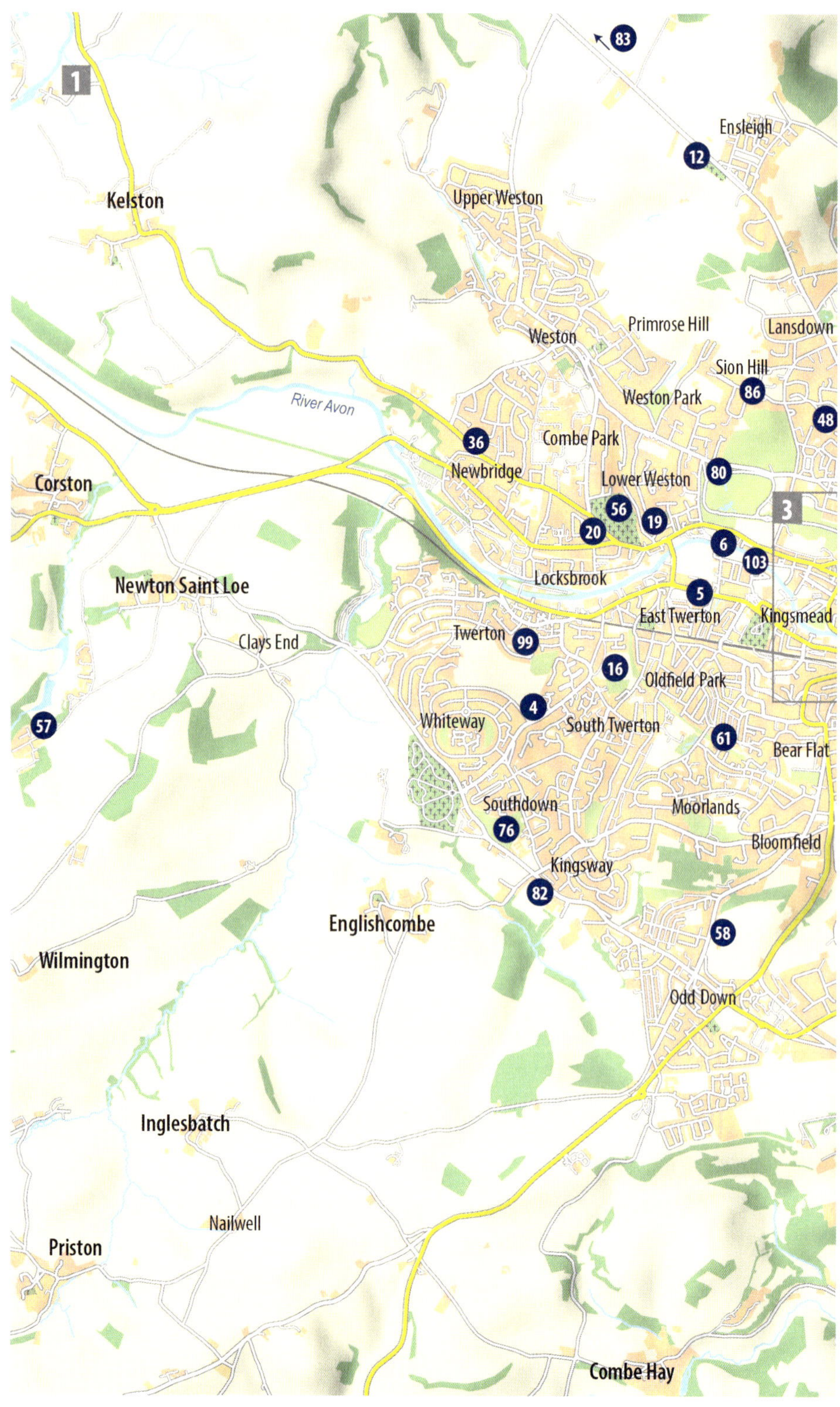
1
83
Ensleigh
12
Kelston
Upper Weston
Primrose Hill
Lansdown
Weston
Sion Hill
86
Weston Park
48
River Avon
36
Combe Park
Newbridge
Lower Weston
80
Corston
56
3
19
20
6
103
Locksbrook
5
Newton Saint Loe
East Twerton
Kingsmead
Twerton
99
Clays End
16
Oldfield Park
4
Whiteway
South Twerton
57
61
Bear Flat
Southdown
Moorlands
76
Bloomfield
Kingsway
82
Englishcombe
58
Wilmington
Odd Down
Inglesbatch
Nailwell
Priston
Combe Hay

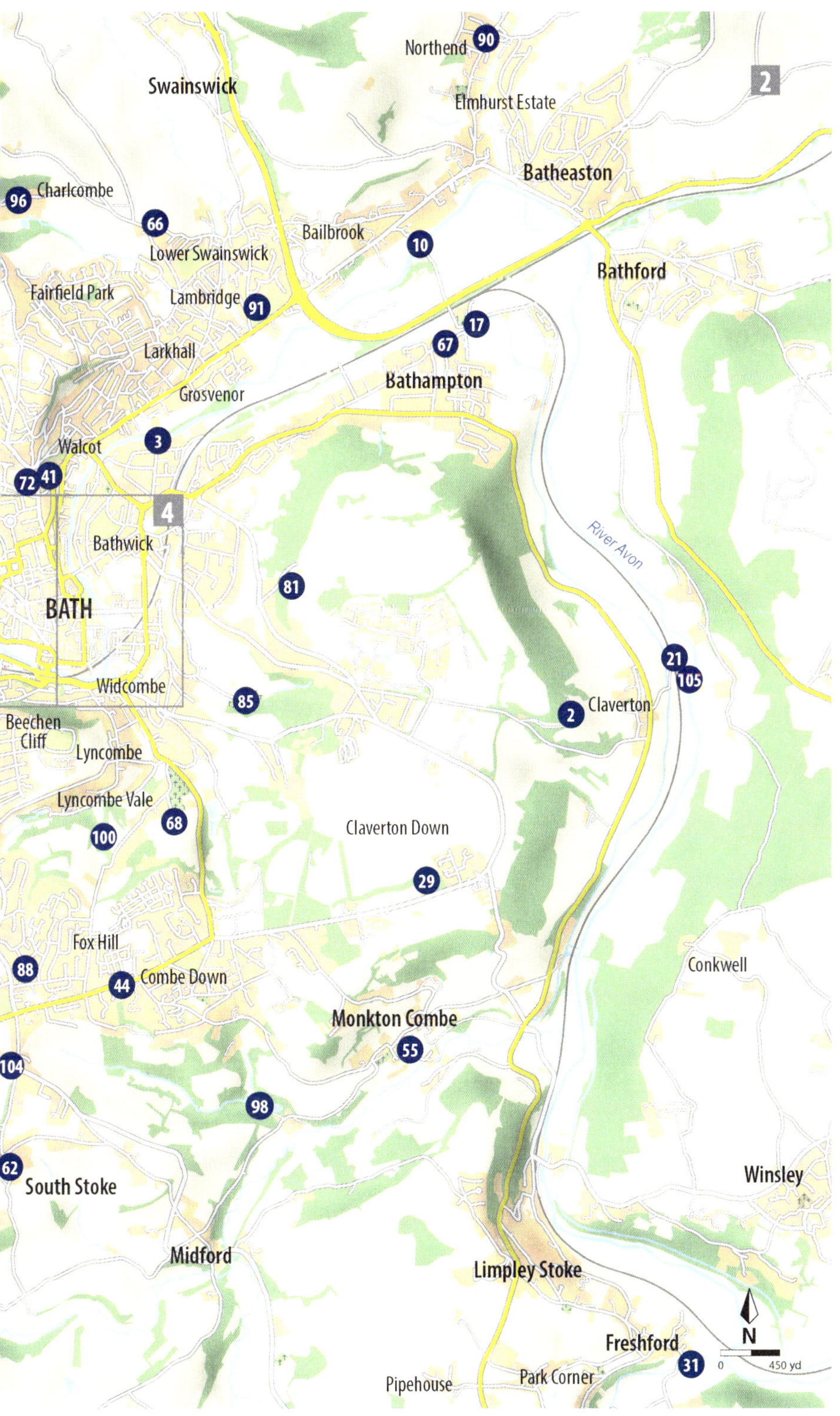

Northend
90
2
Swainswick
Elmhurst Estate
Batheaston
Charlcombe
96
66
Bailbrook
10
Lower Swainswick
Bathford
Fairfield Park
Lambridge
91
17
67
Larkhall
Bathampton
Grosvenor
3
Walcot
72
41
4
Bathwick
River Avon
81
BATH
21
105
Widcombe
85
2
Claverton
Beechen Cliff
Lyncombe
Lyncombe Vale
68
100
Claverton Down
29
Fox Hill
Conkwell
88
44
Combe Down
Monkton Combe
55
104
98
62
South Stoke
Winsley
Midford
Limpley Stoke
N
Freshford
31
0
450 yd
Pipehouse
Park Corner

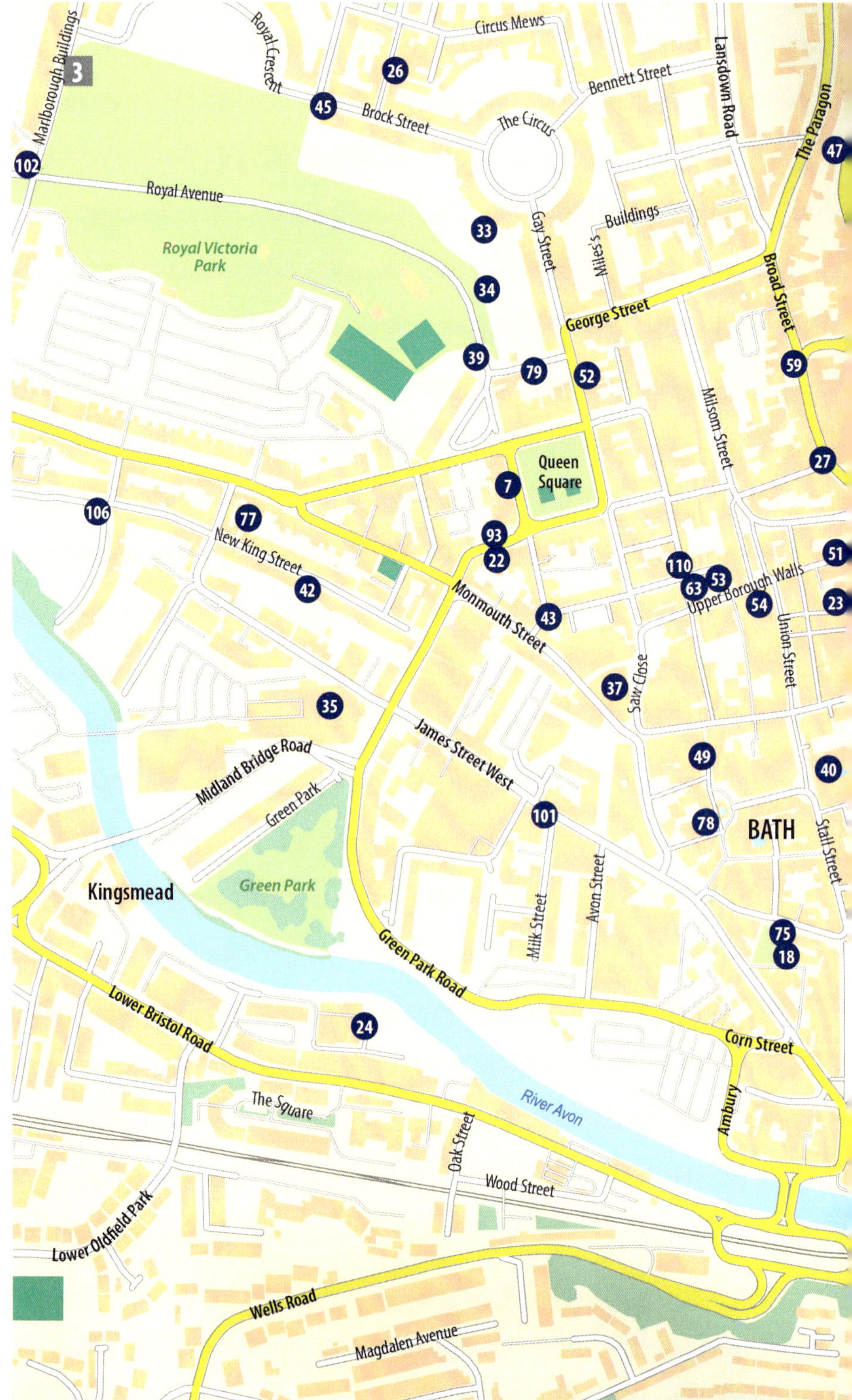

3
Marlborough Buildings
Royal Crescent
Circus Mews
Bennett Street
Lansdown Road
Brock Street
The Circus
The Paragon
Royal Avenue
Miles's Buildings
Gay Street
Royal Victoria Park
Broad Street
George Street
Milsom Street
Queen Square
New King Street
Upper Borough Walls
Monmouth Street
Union Street
Saw Close
James Street West
Midland Bridge Road
Green Park
BATH
Stall Street
Kingsmead
Milk Street
Avon Street
Green Park Road
Corn Street
Lower Bristol Road
River Avon
Ambury
The Square
Oak Street
Wood Street
Lower Oldfield Park
Wells Road
Magdalen Avenue
102
45
26
47
33
34
39
79
52
59
27
7
106
77
93
22
110
53
63
51
54
23
42
43
37
35
49
40
101
78
75
18
24

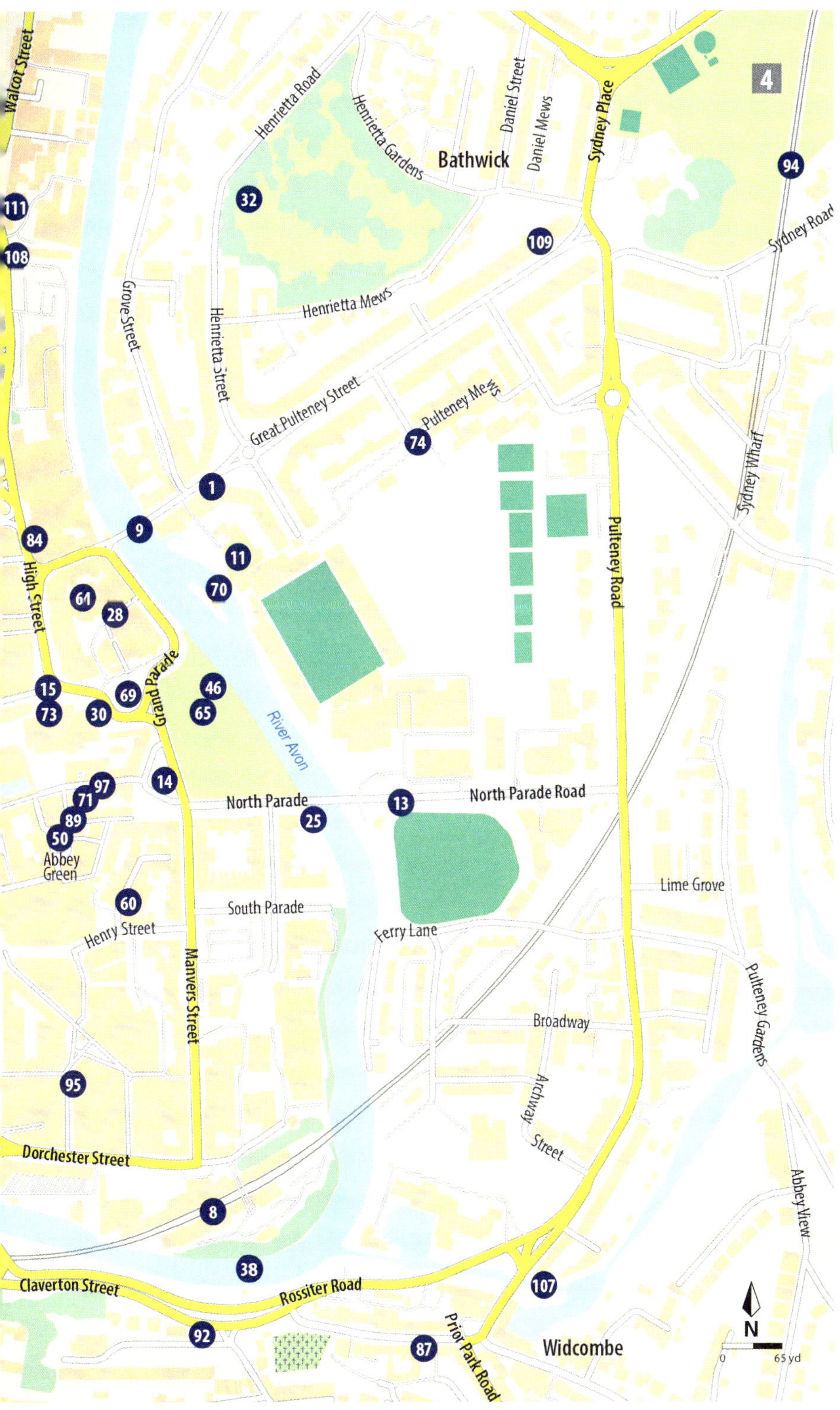
4
Walcot Street
Henrietta Road
Henrietta Gardens
Daniel Street
Daniel Mews
Sydney Place
Bathwick
Sydney Road
Henrietta Mews
Grove Street
Henrietta Street
Great Pulteney Street
Pulteney Mews
Sydney Wharf
Pulteney Road
High Street
Grand Parade
River Avon
North Parade
North Parade Road
Abbey Green
Lime Grove
South Parade
Henry Street
Ferry Lane
Pulteney Gardens
Manvers Street
Broadway
Archway Street
Dorchester Street
Abbey View
Claverton Street
Rossiter Road
Prior Park Road
Widcombe
N
0
65 yd
111
108
32
109
94
74
1
9
84
11
70
61
28
15
73
69
30
46
65
14
97
71
89
50
13
25
60
95
8
38
107
92
87

ACKNOWLEDGEMENTS

This book is dedicated to my amazing wife, Jo. Thank you for being my biggest cheerleader and a constant support by my side. Thank you for the coffees and the stroopwafels, the answers to my grammar questions, and pushing me to achieve more than I ever thought possible. And a huge thank you as well to Mersina and Lois for cycling through tunnels, running parkruns, and exploring bookshops and Roman ruins; even if you did give up finding me when I was in the best hide & seek spot. I wish our adventures can last forever.

Babs: thank you so much! You are the most amazing photographer I could ever hope to work with. To my editor, Ros: thank you for being a calm and guiding hand. To all at Emons, especially Laura: thank you for trusting us again.

Thank you as ever to my mum and dad, Shelagh and Tony, who always encouraged me to explore. To Kai and Amaia: you're in a book! A huge thank you to Sanjit Chudha whose marvellous insight was invaluable. Thanks to Richard Wyatt, whose splendid Bath Newseum website was a constant source of inspiration. And to everyone at Bristol24/7 especially Betty Woolerton and Karen Johnson – sorry for long periods of abandonment and top work for holding the fort admirably in my absence.

Thank you also in no particular order to Philip Bendall, Helen Pugh, John Wimperis, Caroline Stanford, Shawn Naphtali Sobers, Andrew Davison, Thomas Dowson, David Walters, PJ Bendall, Andrew Swift, Mike Macklin, Sheila Hannon, David Workman, Mark Warrick, Jacqueline Burrows, Laszlo Megyesi, the estate of Trevor Fawcett, Clare De-Pulford, Jamie Watkins and Tom Kennedy, Andrew Swift and Kirsten Elliott, Michael Forsyth, Michael Raffael, and Johnny Palmer: gusmeister extraordinaire. Every effort has been made to obtain permission from people to quote their words in this book. I can only apologise to anyone who it has not been possible to contact.

Martin Booth

Huge thanks to Martin & Jo for always being so great to work with and thank you to Emons: our lovely publishers for granting us a third book.

Here are as many thank yous as possible, I apologise if I have left anyone out but be assured I am incredibly grateful for all your support:

Thank you to Mr Doshi & Rajan at AH Pharmacy, Becci at the American Museum, Kat at Bath City Farm, Mike at Bath Stamp & Coin Shop, Alex & Bamboo at Ponte Vecchio, Marie, Sarah & Joe at Beckfords Tower and the Herschel, Kate & Mark at Blowout Sax, Jan at Chapel Arts, Demian at Chapel Forge, Nev at CB Chocolates, the team at Claverton Pumping Station, the team at Colonna & Small's, Oscar & Ian at The Coeur de Lion, Lorna & the team at Dick Willow's, Edward at Bath Abbey, Ras Benji & Emma at Fairfield House, Vicki Smith at Mary Shelley's House of Frankenstein, Ella at Little Theatre Cinema, Daniel & Robin at Magalleria, Sophie at Old Theatre Royal, Msgr Corrigan & Dr Mercer at Our Lady and St Alphege, James at The Packhorse, Saber at Toppings, Graham & Stuart at the Museum of Bath at Work, Iain at the Recreation Ground, Fern at St John's Foundation, Susmita at Shree Jagannatha Temple, Anna at The Small Shop, Lazlo and all at Splasherist, Cheryl and the team at Twerton Park, Matt & Sue at The Urban Garden, Johnny at Warleigh Weir, Mark from Worldbuilders, Clare & Mia from The Yellow Shop, as well as all the lovely people in Bath who I met along the way and shared their stories with me as I went around the city.

Thank you to Ainley, Diana, Paul, Eli, Leo, Jenny and Sangee for giving your time and coming on the journey with me. Thank you to PhotoBath for great conversations over coffee every week.

Finally, thank you to my fab kids, Theo and Anna; Paul for being so supportive; Mum, Anna, Leo, Pete, Carina, Amelia, Artemis and Alma, I'm so lucky to call you my family.

Barbara Evripidou

THE AUTHOR

Martin Booth is a journalist, author and tour guide who lives in Bristol with his wife, Joanna, and their two daughters, Mersina and Lois. He is the Editor of Bristol24/7 and has written for publications including *Time Out, The Guardian* and *Metro.* When not cycling, he can usually be found at a parkrun around the South West and Wales. Follow Martin on Instagram and X for his latest adventures: @beardedjourno

THE PHOTOGRAPHER

Barbara Evripidou is an award-winning photographer with over three decades of experience behind the lens. Beginning her career as a press photographer, her work has appeared in national newspapers, and she has worked extensively across the globe. A defining moment in her career was her time embedded with the British Army in Bosnia, documenting efforts to rebuild the country in the aftermath of conflict. Today, Barbara specialises in PR, portrait and commercial photography, bringing the same depth, sensitivity and storytelling to her subjects. When she's not holding a camera, she can be found at a metal gig or exploring her home city of Bristol, where she lives with her children Theo and Anna, and partner Paul.
Find out more at firstavenuephotography.com.

The information in this book was accurate at the time of publication, but it may change at any time. Please confirm the details for the places you're planning to visit before you head out on your adventures.